THE INTEGRATION

OF

HUMAN VALUES

Cornelius J. van der Poel, C.S.Sp.

Dimension Books · Denville, New Jersey

Copyright © 1977

Cornelius J. van der Poel

ISBN 0-87193-004-8

First English Edition

Published by Dimension Books, Inc.

Denville, New Jersey, 07834

TABLE OF CONTENTS

INTRODUCTION

Our present era is filled with apparent contradictions. To mention only a few: the need for deep communication on a personal level is considered more and more an absolute necessity for the emotional well-being of every individual; yet, social isolation seems to be steadily increasing. The need for community involvement is continuously stressed; at the same time there seems to be a constant increase of individualism to the point of egotism. The present generation knows better than at any other time in history the importance of a concerned and loving family relationship in the formation of a balanced personality; yet, at no time in history has the family been more unstable than today. Never before in history has there been so much power and technical ability in the hands of men; yet, never before has the human race experienced greater insecurity. Vatican Council II pointed out that present day development of human sciences has a deep impact upon religious values. This impact brings many persons to a deeper personal faith; yet, the explicit rejection of religion in all its expressions is increasing alarmingly. (Gaudium et Spes. n. 7)

One gets the impression that humanity is searching desperately for the meaning and value of its own existence. Developing technology seems to suggest to some that human science will eventually master the source of its own being. Humanity's constant experience of limitations suggests a power beyond the human at its origin. The unanswerable question of existence itself demands a source of origin which escapes all human comprehension and calculation. Many people search for an answer in a personal relationship with God. Only in the acceptance-in-faith of a God who creates and communicates life can we begin to fully respect the universe and all that it contains.

With regard to human life and human existence, Vatican Council II says: "Only in the mystery of the Incarnate Word does the mystery of man take on light." This means that faith in creation and redemption is the only perspective in which the human being can be fully accepted. Created in the image of God, the human being remains a mystery. It is a mystery which begins to make sense only when we see human existence in the light of God's creative and redemptive self-giving.

The Vatican Council refers to the mystery of the Incarnate Word as a means for understanding the mystery of human existence. In this way the Council speaks of the total unity of the human and the divine in one person, Jesus, who mysteriously unites the finite with the infinite. The Council presents this same mysterious unity as the form and norm for understanding the complexity and wholeness of the human reality. It is as if the Council wants to avoid the idea of layers in which the finite and infinite dimensions are somehow brought together. The Council seems to teach that without integration of these seeming opposites there is no human wholeness.

The search for this full integration is the subject of this book. It is not the author's intention to give an answer. Any real integration cannot be outlined on paper. It can only be lived in the faith-filled reality of human existence. It is, however, the author's opinion that every human being, because he/she is created in God's image, must bring the reality of God's life to a personal experience in his/her own way of living. To live the life of God and to share in the life of God is possible only in the active expression of the human personality.

The human response to God has no predetermined outline. Each person in his/her own way participates in God's love and gives visible expression to God's creative love and goodness. The communication of God's life to every individual human being does not occur apart from the everyday reality of each individual. This means that the way a person or personality is, is the way in which he/she will receive God's life and respond to it. Nature and grace become one principle of operation.

The response to daily life and the response to God are not two different things. In daily life a person responds to God, either in faith, through denial or by indifference, and this response to God influences one's daily behavior. The human personality structure provides the form in which the life of God either expresses itself or is denied in the human reality of this individual. Similarly, participation in the life of God or the denial of God's presence will influence the structure and development of the personality.

It has always been an aspect of Christian teaching that Christian virtues are a dynamic reality in human existence. However, certain religious/devotional (perhaps super-stitious) practices have sometimes been presented as virtues. This tendency has made many people hesitant to speak about virtues. Thus the virtues which are both human dynamics and God's gift are often not studied. Yet, it seems to be quite important to understand some of the dynamics of the human response to God.

If the human being is called to share in the life of God, then the proper development of human potential and the proper response to God must coincide. This means that the way a person has developed is also the way in which a person responds to God. This must also be the way in which the virtues are formed and grow. This present work searches for the integration of the personality structure and the Christian virtues.

Sometimes these pages may give the impression that virtues flow forth from psychological structures and development. It is never the author's intention to present such an opinion. On the contrary, the author believes very firmly that the sharing in God's life is a special gift of God to the individual. He also believes that this gift does not hover above or outside of the human reality, but that it is integrated within the personality structure and can be seen and experienced only through the personality. Consequently, the better we understand the personality structure, the better we can understand the person's relationship with God, and the better we can assist when a person appeals to us for guidance. The stress on the personality structure is always meant to approach the person in his/her relationship with God.

The present text is a result of countless hours of reflection and prayer, guidance, discussion and teaching. It has been presented as a course to College students, to students in Masters programs for Religious Education, to priests and to laity. It has always had one purpose, to search for ways to integrate the finite and the infinite in the human reality. It is a search for the reality of God in human life, and for the human participation in the life of God. It is the author's prayer that all who read these pages may come to a deeper understanding of their own personality and so respond more generously to the God who creates and redeems.

ACKNOWLEDGEMENT

I want to take this opportunity to express my most sincere gratitude to the many friends who contributed to the development of my thoughts. I want to mention particularly many students at Viterbo College in La Crosse, Wisconsin; participants in summer programs at Duquesne University, Pittsburgh, Pennsylvania, and at St. Michael's College in Winooski, Vermont; Parishioners at St. Rene's parish in Sterling Heights, Michigan; priest-friends who came together with me at Sacred Heart Seminary in Detroit, Michigan; teams of parish-ministers (priests, religious and laity) who studied with me to search for ways to bring God's life and God's love to their people. Their encouragements and disagreements, their discussions, questions and clarifications have made it possible to formulate these concepts.

Further I want to express my sincere thanks to Revs. James Coombs, S.S.E. at St. Michael's College, Winooski, Vermont; Michael O'Leary, St. Jude's parish, Detroit; John McGrail, S.J. St. Peter and Paul parish, Detroit; Srs. Mary Agnes Ryan, I.H.M. Detroit and Patricia Foley, S.S.J. Warren, Michigan, for reading and critiquing the manuscript. To Srs. Virginia Sullivan and Mary Agnes Ryan for their painstaking efforts to correct grammar and style. Finally to Irene Skarjune in Livonia, Michigan for doing the typing. Without their continuous encouragement and assistance this work would never have been accomplished.

Cornelius J. van der Poel, C.S.Sp.

1. THE SEARCH FOR INTEGRATION

The increasing knowledge of psychology, of technology and of other sciences which relate to human existence seems to push the importance of God and of the spiritual dimensions of human life to the background. Yet there is a tendency among the younger generation as well as among the older generation to search for values which go beyond the visible and the tangible. Without saying it in so many words, many people feel that human life without values beyond the perceptible is incomplete.

For people who believe in God this tendency of searching for values beyond the perceptible is quite natural. In one form or another they express the faith that God created the human being. People who accept the Scriptures believe what is said in the Book of Genesis (1:27): "God created man in the image of himself, in the image of God he created him." Thus they accept at the very origin of their life a power which is beyond their control and beyond their comprehension, yet this power lies at the heart of their being.

To be created by God means to be totally dependent on God. To accept this dependence impresses upon human beings that their way of behaving is not completely their own. The goal of human existence is related to its origin and is, therefore, established by the creator.

The usual description of the concept of 'creating' is "to

make something out of nothing''. It is a very valid effort to describe simultaneously the power of the creator and total human dependence. This same description also has certain disadvantages. To make something out of nothing suggests a relationship of craftsman to artifact. It is a relationship which is comparable to a sculptor-statue relationship, or to an artist-painting relationship.

In each of these relationships the greatness of the maker will be manifested, and many qualities of the personality of the artist will be revealed. A painting not only shows the artistic ability but also the artist's sensitivity to form, composition, light, moods, etc. But however great the amount of information may be which is conveyed by the painting, it remains information *about* the artist. It does not convey the life of the artist. We often speak about creative art in which an artist expresses the inner depths of his/her personality in a new and visible manner. In isolated instances the painting may give inspiration to those who admire it, yet, by and large the painting remains mostly ''the work of his hands''.

The communication of personality and life is slightly more visible in the author who expresses his inner thoughts and feelings in the book that he published. The following example may help us to understand better what I mean. A couple of years ago, while I was walking on a university campus on my way to the lecture hall where I had to give an address, two priests were walking a few steps behind me. Both were teachers of theology in a college. They were discussing the book which they had selected as the basic text for their course. I could not help overhearing every word they said, and they did not know that I was the author of that book.

It is a very humbling (not humiliating) experience to hear one's own thoughts and visions expressed in a very different way. In their conversation one of them said: "What the author really means is . . . " and the other elaborated on this revised expression. My first inclination was to turn around and ask them "Why don't you say it this way (my way), that is much clearer." However something held me back and after a few moments, I realized that my own insights were being translated into their minds and personalities. My insights had not lost anything of their value or of their accuracy, but they were re-expressed in a manner in which I could not express them. My insights were not just empty concepts in their new expression, rather, they showed a richness of which I was not aware. In a certain way I became part of these men's conviction and life without losing anything of myself. Their enrichment became my enrichment too. The book which I had published was not anymore a simple "work of my hands", but a communication of life and person. This little incident made me more deeply aware of the role and of the meaning of the creator who not simply "made" the human being so that God could be recognized in the artifact, but who communicates constantly his own life and person.

Perhaps a still clearer understanding of the communication of life in creation may be obtained when we compare the act of creation with the work of a composer. The music which is written does not only express the skill of the composer, but first and foremost it expresses the mood of the composer, the depth and quality of his feelings. Without separating himself from his feelings, the composer places them, as it were, outside himself and brings them within the reach of other people. Now other persons can reproduce the feelings of the composer and bring them to life by playing his music.

This reproduction demands in the first place that the musician himself develop musical skills. The better a musician is able to play a certain instrument the more accurately the feelings of the composer can be reproduced. If a reproduction is accurate, it is possible to recognize the feelings of the composer. The better the reproduction, the more completely the composer will come to life.

At the same time the life and the feelings of the musician penetrate every dimension of the reproduction. The life and the feelings of the composer and of the musician remain two different realities, but at this particular moment they are so intimately intertwined that the one cannot be observed without the other. The composer is recognized in the musician's expression. The better the musician's musical skills are developed, the more completely will the musician's personality be fulfilled and the more perfectly will the composer's feelings be re-expressed.

Elsewhere I have tried to explain how the musician must stay within the writings of the composer otherwise the composer's feelings and life will not be reproduced.[1] There is no need to repeat these points here. For our present purpose it is sufficient to keep the following points in mind.

a. When the music is played, the feelings of the composer and the musician are so intertwined that at this moment the one cannot be recognized without the other, yet they remain two different realities.

b. The more the musician succeeds in grasping the feelings of the composer the more perfect the reproduction will be.

c. "Living into" the feelings of the composer does not mean a loss of the musician's personality. On the contrary, it opens new depth-dimensions for the musician.

d. Although the musician tries to grasp the composer's feelings, it remains unavoidable that the

expression of the composer's feelings is strongly
influenced by the personality and by the feelings
of the musician. It would even be accurate to say
that the composer's feelings blend together with
the musician's feelings. Or perhaps we should say
that the composer allows himself to be expressed
through the personality of the musician without
loss of personality and dignity in either one.

The elaboration on this example is intended to refine
our understanding of creation as a "self-communication of
God to the creature". This self-communication is not a
power display, but a reaching out which is life-giving so
that God's life is expressed in created limitations, but
nonetheless complete and real.

The example of the composer and the musician gives
us a further insight. The composer's life and feelings are
expressed in the form of the musician's personality. Some
musicians may be able to express the composer's feelings
with greater accuracy than others because of their highly
developed skills and because of the structure of their
personalities. Certain personality-structures or certain
emotional conditions are unable to grasp or to express
certain compositions. A person in a very depressed mood
cannot fully express the joys of the "Halleluia" of Handel's
Messiah. Either the musician's sadness will tint the
reproduction of the Halleluia and distort it, or the joys of
the Halleluia will change the mood of the musician.

In this example I am trying to point out how in human
life outside influences—we may say transcendent
dimensions—are translated into the human personality,
and how the human personality is influenced by transcendent dimensions. In this mutual influence the human
person can develop constructively. This will mean an accurate expression of the transcendent and a gain for the

human being. A person can also distort a transcendent dimension. This would mean an inaccurate presentation of the transcendent and a loss for the personality.

When we transfer these ideas to human life and its relationship to God then we may be able to understand more deeply the meaning of creation. The self-communication of God's own life to the human being is not an addition to an already existing human reality. Rather it is a dimension which belongs to human life and which makes the human being fully human.

This same understanding helps us also to see the importance of the personality structure for the human participation in the life of God. Just as the composer's feelings are expressed according to the personality and to the ability of the musician, so also is the expression of God's life in humanity influenced by the personality structure of individual human beings. Just as the musician's feelings and personality can be influenced by the feelings of the composer, so also can the personality structure of the believer be influenced by the participation in God's life. The human personality and the divine self-communication must integrate into a "one-ness" and into a "wholeness" in order to have a "total human being" created "in the image of God".

It is a very common saying that grace builds upon nature. This statement expresses at least two important aspects in the human relationship with God. First it says that God's presence with the individual—the individual's participation in the life of God—is not independent of the human setting in time and space. Further it says that the life of God and human existence in this world are not the same thing. Although it is true that God created the human being in the image of God and that, therefore, it belongs to human existence (through God's gift) to participate in the life of God, this participation is not a claim of created existence, but remains totally God's gift.

That grace builds upon nature is a very important truth, but one must be careful not to understand it as if we are dealing with different layers which somehow are attached to each other. Grace—God's self-giving to the human—is a gift which is not an addition to an already existing wholeness. It is a reality which penetrates the human reality, and by integrating itself with the human reality, it brings a wholeness to the human being. It elevates the created existence to a level which simultaneously is the goal of the human being and, yet, it is beyond the created claim of any individual. No human being can *demand* a participation in the life of God.

When I speak about the integration of human values, I do not want to place grace-God's life with the human—on the same level as the created reality. Human wholeness includes a participation in the life of God, yet this participation remains completely God's free gift to the human. This free gift, however, is expressed through the activation of the human potential.

The search for integration is, therefore, a search for the various dimensions of human development. It is a study of the human personality in so far as the structure of the personality provides the form and shape in which God's life and love will manifest itself in a specific individual. It includes also the study of how the personal relationship with God influences the development of the personality structure. For example, the form and the degree in which an individual accepts him/herself and others will strongly influence this individual's relationship to God. On the other hand, the individual's (strong) faith in God and in God's goodness will deepen and strengthen the person's self-image.

In the context of the search for integration there seem to be three dimensions or aspects of the human personality which are very important for the constructive self-expression of the human reality. First there is the person in his/her social relationships. Interaction with other persons is essential in human development. This interpersonal development, perhaps more accurately called psycho-socio-development, is a slow process. Each previous stage sets the tone for each subsequent stage and influences the direction of its development. To understand the successive stages through which a person goes in a normal developmental process can be very helpful for a better understanding how this person is likely to react to other persons and to God. Not as if God's grace depends on the personality-structure, but grace will express itself largely through the structure of the personality.

Secondly, there is the aspect of mental health. This is closely related to the structure of the personality, but it is not the same. Mental health cannot be properly defined, however, there are certain criteria which should be present in the greater or lesser degree when a person is mentally healthy. These criteria manifest themselves more or less according to the stages of the psycho-socio development. It is not as if a specific criteria is a characteristic of a certain stage of development, but a certain criterion may find its form and direction more clearly in a specific stage of psycho-socio relationships. The relationship with God, particularly the holiness of a person, does not depend on the degree of mental health. Obviously, a person must be capable of personal responsibility, but holiness is not restricted to mental health. [2] On the other hand, a person's relationship with God is largely shaped according to one's intellectual and emotional way of being.

The third important aspect is what we might call the

"ethical modality". The structure of the personality together with the balance of insight and emotions create in a person an inclination and feeling of what is good and acceptable, or what is not acceptable. This does not necessarily coincide with a moral law. It is rather a sensing of what seems to be constructive or destructive for his/her personality. However intimately this dimension may be related to the psycho-socio stage of development and to the stages of mental health, it is not the same. The sense of constructive or destructive value is not a necessary consequence of the other two stages, yet it is closely related to them.

This stage or this dimension is also very closely related to the individual's relationship with God. Not only will commandments be evaluated in the perspective of this ethical modality, but also the interhuman relationships will largely be judged according to these norms. This personal inclination is not always in accordance with the laws of God or of the Church. If there is a coincidence between God's laws and the personal inclinations it will be easy to accept God's laws. If there is a discrepancy there may be a problem. On the other hand, a deepening relationship with God through faith or through any other virtue will be invaluable for re-directing one's personal inclinations.

These three aspects together: the psycho-socio developmental stages, the degree of the criteria for mental health, and the ethical modality form, as it were, the human being whom we meet every day. It is the human being without the perspective of the divine grace—it is the human being whom we can observe.

Undoubtedly, divine grace works in every dimension of this existence, but it may not be identified with any of these aspects. It does not flow forth from any of them, because it is totally beyond any created claim. Nonetheless, it expresses itself through these dimensions and in the form of these dimensions. At the same time it helps shape, develop and mature these dimensions and leads them to a form of wholeness which is entirely human and which forms the human completeness, yet which is beyond the claim of the created. To be fully human remains God's gift.

Thus we have a fourth dimension in our search for integration of human values, namely, the Christian virtues. Virtues do not flow forth from the other dimensions, yet, they do not exist in the individual without them. Virtues do not create the other dimensions, yet, they contribute to their development. Virtues are shaped by the other dimensions, and conversely, they help shape these dimensions. There is a continuous interplay between the self-expression of the creature and the self-communication of the creator to the creature. This interplay makes the human being fully human. It expresses the visible self-manifestation of the creator through the human limitations, and leads to the real integration of human values.

In an effort to deepen our understanding of the interaction of these four dimensions of the integrated human existence, I want to study in the following chapters each individual dimension and its interaction with the other dimensions. This study may give the impression that spiritual life is primarily approached from a psychological point of view. In reality, however, it is an effort to understand the human person to greater depth. The interaction of these four dimensions can show how the development of this personality can strengthen the life of virtue, and how growth in virtue can enhance the development of the personality.

In order to build up slowly to the full vision of integration each individual dimension will be related only to the dimensions which have been studied earlier. For instance, the psycho-socio stages will be studied on their own, the criteria for mental health will be studied on their own and in comparison with the psycho-socio stages, the ethical modalities will be studied on their own and in their relationship with the other two. Finally, the Christian virtues will first be studied on their own and then in their relationship with the previously studied dimensions. At the end of each chapter there will be charts indicating the relationships in which each item has been studied until that point.

2. DEVELOPMENTAL STRUCTURES OF THE HUMAN PERSONALITY

It is our strongest belief that the human being and the human personality originates at the moment of conception. From that moment on we have a separate human existence which deserves the full respect for human life. The physical and psychological incompleteness or the total dependence of such an early human being do not diminish its human dignity.

It is obvious, however, that at this early stage the human qualities of being and personality are hardly recognizable. Without underestimating the human dignity we can speak more accurately of a potentiality for these qualities than of their presence. These potentialities develop (or perhaps unfold) into recognizable human qualities. This unfolding itself is a continuous process which does not stop as long as the human being is alive in this world.

The unfolding of the potential into recognizable qualities is not a juxtaposition of independent qualities. It is a growing process in which each step depends largely upon the previous stage of development, and is greatly influenced by external circumstances. There is a mutual interaction between various developmental stages. We may say that perfection is (in potentiality) present in the most primitive stage of growth and influences the direction of the growth. On the other hand, the most primitive stages of development continue to influence the developmental process of later stages.

The human being is by nature a social being who needs certain forms of interhuman relationships in order to reach full human maturity. This means that a human being needs to reach out of himself in order to become fully himself. This human need to reach out in order to be complete is an important point to keep in mind with regard to religious development. In religious development a person reaches out to God and accepts God's reaching out to him. Religious development is very closely related to interpersonal relationships. This is reflected in the words of the Scripture: "By this love you have for one another, everyone will know that you are my disciples. (Jn. 13:35)" And elsewhere, "A man who does not love the brother that he can see cannot love God, whom he has never seen. (1 Jn. 4:20)" Therefore, the developmental structures of the personality which are important in the human relationships with God are the same basic structures which are important for interhuman relationships.

Psychological sciences have made many efforts to describe the human personality in its various stages of growth and development. I don't think that any one of them claims completeness or infallibility. There is always a groping in search for the human mystery. It would seem that among the various possible approaches the theory of Erik Erikson about the psycho-socio crises in human development comes closest to our purpose. Erik Erikson points to eight stages of psycho-socio development.[1] These stages are mutually interrelated, although they appear more explicitly at certain age levels. At each stage, from childhood to old age, the study is concerned with the person's interhuman relationships.

These developmental stages of the human personality provide a form in which the human relationship with God can express itself. For this reason we need to study them in some detail. In very concise terms we can state them as follows.

6. Basic Trust vs. Basic Mistrust.
   This first stage relates to the degree in which a newborn child feels accepted by its surrounding for its own personal value.
2. Autonomy vs. Shame or Doubt.
   This stage is concerned with the development of the motor-functions. The child experiences itself as a source of activity and tests out its acceptability by the surrounding adults.
3. Initiative vs. Guilt.
   It is the stage of the fantasy world which is acted out in earnest play. The rejection of actions and play is experienced as a personal rejection.
4. Industry vs. Inferiority.
   It is the stage in which the child wants to learn and experience personal acceptability by the surrounding adults.
5. Identity vs. Identity diffusion.
   The rapid growth of the adolescent triggers a whole new search for an acceptable relationship with oneself and with the outside.
6. Intimacy vs. Isolation.
   A newly found identity can be a proud discovery which one wants to share with others. It also can be a frightening realization which makes one withdraw from others.
7. Generativity vs. Stagnation & Self-Absorption.
   The desire to share with others contains the desire to communicate of one's own life. The fear to be known

inhibits progress and creates a disproportionate concern for self.

8. Integrity vs. Despair or Disgust.

   By positive development the human qualities fuse into a oneness of expression which gives happiness and fulfillment. A defective development creates an undue groping and unhappiness with oneself.

The above description is too elementary to be useful by itself alone. In the following pages of this chapter I will elaborate on each individual stage. The purpose of this elaboration is not primarily an analytical process to investigate origin and consequences. My purpose is rather to present a descriptive picture of how these stages contribute to the form of self-expression of the personality.

The brief description that is given here indicates already in a very general manner that all the stages are very closely related. Particularly every previous stage provides the major basis upon which later stages are developed. However, in the process of later development many disadvantages of earlier stages can be corrected.

The use of the word "versus" in each of the psycho-socio crises must not be misunderstood. It does not indicate a continuous battle between two extremes, such as between a trust and mistrust of certain individuals. It rather points to a degree of balance. For instance, trust and mistrust form two poles of a tension. Between these poles the individual develops a certain balance with which he/she feels comfortable. It means, too, a simultaneous presence of a certain degree of self-acceptance as well as a certain degree of self-doubt. The word "versus" is more a dynamic balancing than a mutual exclusivity.[2] Let us now try to elaborate on the meaning of the developmental stages.

Basic Trust vs. Basic Mistrust

This first stage is the stage of infancy and covers approximately the period from birth to one year of age. Its main concern is the infant's relationship in the transition from intrauterine life to the interaction with other persons. It is also concerned with the awakening of self-awareness. The infant which is hardly aware of a personal existence distinct from the cosmic surrounding begins to recognize itself, in however an elementary way, as an individual in its own right. Both aspects of transition have an enormous impact upon the life of the infant and present real crises.

The intrauterine life is perhaps the closest to a perfect equilibrium that can be imagined. There is little (if any) experience of needs. There is no hunger, no thirst, no need for a bath. This almost perfect condition, however, is discontinued suddenly and violently at the moment of birth. The infant, not even aware of its own separate existence, is subjected to a flood of stimuli which are totally alien. The infant has no means of coping with these stimuli and experiences them as threatening. There is in the infant a continuous search for a condition which comes as close as possible to the state of equilibrium which was experienced in the intrauterine life. The experiences of hunger, thirst and the need for cleaning thrust the infant constantly back to the feeling of complete helplessness and total dependence.

Where the experience of personal helplessness and the response of the environment begin to interact, the infant begins to experience the degree in which it feels personally accepted or not accepted. Obviously, there is no reasoning process through which the infant can draw conclusions, yet the infant experiences and recognizes the quality of love that is given. Somehow and in ways which we do not understand, the infant senses whether it is accepted for its own sake and value or for the benefit of someone else. In certain instances it may experience that it is not accepted at all.

It may happen that there is no rejection on the part of the parents but circumstances beyond their control make it impossible to provide the care which the infant seems to ask. Other children who demand attention may prevent their devoting much time to the infant. The poor health of the infant may prevent the desired equilibrium despite all the efforts of the parents.

When the child experiences a care and concern which provides the desired equilibrium, it is more likely to develop a sense of personal acceptability. To the degree that this equilibrium is lacking, the infant is likely to develop a feeling that it is not acceptable or wanted. This feeling is the basis for the infant's concept of personal value or of the lack of it. In the infant develops a certain balance. To a degree it can trust its surroundings as loving and accepting or to a degree it cannot trust its surroundings.

There is hardly any doubt that this basic approach to human interaction can change in future development, particularly when a person begins to understand what happened to him/her in the earlier periods. At this early stage, however, the infant's approach to interhuman exchange is based upon the balance of the moment. The early balance forms a basic attitude in further development.

Autonomy vs. Shame or Doubt

The second stage of development covers roughly the period from one to three years of age. This stage is mostly concerned with the development of the motor-functioning of the child. During this period a child begins to walk and to climb on furniture. It begins to explore the various parts of the house and it reaches for things in order to subject them to closer scrutiny.

This period is a development in a very different direction than the former one. The search for balance between personal acceptability and the lack of it, which characterized the former period, is mainly concerned about a personal value. Though unconsciously, it is a self-evaluation through the degree of acceptance which is experienced through others. In a certain sense, it is the person turning into him/herself.

In this second period the individual researches its relationship with other persons. The fact that a child begins to walk is much more than a physical phenomenon. It is also a very important psychological (and emotional) experience. Until that time the infant was dependent on others for every change of locality. Now it can achieve this on its own power and initiative. By this time there is a very vivid awareness in the child of its own existence separate from the rest of the world. With this awakening awareness there is also an irresistible curiosity to explore other beings (or things). Such explorations may often lead to conflict situations with adults or with other siblings.

The form of autonomy which the child develops during this period will be a combination between the personal needs to utilize his/her own motor functions and satisfy his/her curiosity, and the acceptability of this self-activation by the surrounding. When the child feels that its activities are accepted by the surrounding adults, or that at least there is an accepting guidance into the activation of its potential, the child will experience a personal value. If the activation of its potential is a source of anger in the adults, the child will feel a lack of personal value. At this stage of development the child cannot distinguish between rejection of its activity and personal rejection. A rejection of its activity means to the child a personal rejection.

The constant rejection of the child's activity causes a feeling of personal no-goodness, a feeling of shame and of doubt about itself. This period is also considered to be extremely important for the development of cooperation with others. Erikson says that "this period will be decisive for the ratio between love and hate, between cooperation and willfulness and between the freedom of self-expression and its suppression". [3]

The basic thrust of this period is the child's search for "personal value in relation to others". The newly discovered powers, the motor functioning as well as anal control, provide an opportunity for cooperation or opposition. The balance between these two becomes part of the child's self-image with regard to others. Although this second stage is not the same as the first, it seems obvious that there is a close relationship between the two. The child who experiences a feeling of acceptance will easily accept guidance. The child who never felt acceptance will most likely experience every adult intervention as a threat to its own personality. Such a child will defend itself accordingly, either by withdrawing from activity or by secretive acting. Moreover, the persons (parents) who did not accept the child at the earlier stage will probably have little patience with its (annoying) activities.

Initiative vs. Guilt

The third stage is called the stage of the play-age and covers approximately the period between three and six years of age. During this time the child lives very much in its own world of fantasy. Hands and feet function well enough, they don't need attention. At the former stage they demanded the mind's attention, now they are at the service of the mind.

The capacity to observe the behavior of others and the use of instruments and objects stimulates toward imitation in the child's own way. The imitation is frequently a new creation. To the adult it seems that the youngster plays a game but for the child the play has a seriousness which borders on a reality. During the earlier stages the child has discovered its personal value, i.e. the degree in which it experiences itself as valuable in its own eyes because it feels accepted in the eyes of others. Further it has discovered to what extent it is allowed to reach out on its own initiative. These two opposite directions, the self-directedness and the other directedness of earliest childhood, are now brought together into one expression. In a very literal sense the child puts itself into its play.

If the surrounding world accepts this self-expression and respects the initiative of the youngster the child's self-image is confirmed and strengthened. If the self-expression is rejected it means for the child a personal rejection. Among other instances this can be very concretely observed in the little boy or girl who wants to marry mommy or daddy or an aunt or an uncle. The little girl who says that she wants to marry daddy or a favored uncle is not really playing. She is serious. It is her way of saying that she wants to be meaningful to this person, to love him and to be loved by him. To punish her because of such a statement, to reproach her for it or to ignore it, is a very personal rejection. If such a rejection is experienced only once it may not be too important. If it is part of a pattern this attitude of rejection will easily create an uncomfortable tension in the youngster.

Such a tension is apt to create a guilt feeling in a child.

This guilt-feeling is a very personal experience. It is the feeling of being personally rejectable or bad because of the activity in which she was engaged or because of the words which she said. It contains a very strange and severe tension because the child experiences rejection for doing something which was meant to be so good.

Rejection or acceptance in the area of being boy or girl is particularly important because of its contribution to the future self-image as man or as woman. The individual's self-concept has a great influence upon future behavior. In many instances the experiences of this period are closely related to the experiences of the earlier stages. The child who felt accepted during the preconscious stages of its being, and who felt the freedom to develop its own tendencies to move and to explore, is much less apt to feel rejected than the child who had opposite experiences.

A child who had negative experiences in the earliest stages of life and who now finds these negative feelings confirmed by conscious experiences (imagined or real) of rejection will find it very difficult to approach life in a trusting manner. On the other hand, a real trusting and positive attitude of the adult world at this stage can even correct many unfortunate experiences of the earlier stages.

Industry vs. Inferiority

The fourth stage of development coincides more or less with the school-age of the child. It covers the period of approximately six to twelve years of age. It begins with the time that a child begins to outgrow its own fantasy world. Not as if the child stops fantasizing, but it begins to discover that reality is important and that it does not always coincide with fantasy. It is the development of a need to prove one's personal value by the things that one can do.

Erikson tries to capture the essence and the differences

of the first four stages in the following brief assessment.
' "At the first stage the personality crystallizes around the
conviction 'I am what I am given', that of the second 'I am
what I will." The third can be characterized by 'I am what I
can imagine I will be,' and the fourth "I am what I learn."[4]

At this age-level success becomes very important, but
it is not simply the success in the sense of material
achievement. One of the major aspects of success is the
experience of being personally acceptable by important
persons in one's life *because of one's work.* Encouragement
and praise are indispensable elements during this period of
development, but they must be honest. The combination of
initiative and industry must have a goal outside the child
itself. This means that there must be important persons in
the child's life whose favor is won or strengthened by the
work ~~that is being done~~. ~~Educators often noti~~ce how the
~~child~~'s ~~marks go down when relationshi~~ps at home
deteriorate.

~~This period is also the beginning~~ of a more concrete
form of competition. This competition has a variety of
consequences. It can convey the understanding (experience) that he/she is not the center of the world. There
are others against whom one must compete, and with whom
one must cooperate. It contains the development of a social
dimension and of a mutual respect in giving and taking
beyond the limits of the immediate family. However important this development of social awareness may be, it
remains necessary to retain and to display a respect for the
individual as individual even if competitions are constantly
lost.

Since this period is characterized by the two interrelated dimensions of consciousness and learning, it is
also of major importance for the formation of a social
conscience. Consequently, this period is also very important

for the religious formation and for the formation of a moral conscience.

Identity vs. Identity Diffusion

After the school-age the youngster enters into the period of adolescence. Even the thought of this stage of development provokes many negative feelings in adults who must deal with these young people. This stage is often described as a time of turmoil and rebellion. Perhaps it may also be described as a period of challenge for the young people who are involved.

Adolescence is a time of many important changes in the life of every human being. Although these changes have been in preparation for a long time, it seems as if they come out of nowhere without any forewarning. Almost suddenly the bodily proportions change from a childhood appearance to the expression of the young adult. The apparent tranquility of the latency period seems abruptly disturbed by the awakening of sexual urges. The relatively quiet acceptance of dependence on home and parents makes place for a resistance to authority and a fight for independence. There are three major aspects—physical appearance, personality relationships, and personal independence—which bring new and alien dimensions to the life of the young person.

With all these changes going on, it is understandable that the young person hardly recognizes him/herself. There is a real identity crisis in which he/she must find a personal value and a place which is very different from the earlier and familiar situation. There is need for an integration of all former experiences into this one new condition. This integration is not a sum-total of earlier identifications. It is rather the accruement—the integrating growth—of the earlier experiences. In the earlier experiences there was a balance of the alignments of the individual's basic drives with his/her endowments and opportunities. The sense of ego identity will be there "when there is an accrued confidence that one's ability to maintain inner sameness and continuity is matched by the sameness and continuity of one's meaning for others."[5]

Obviously, before this new balance of self-acceptance and the new relational dimensions fall into place, there is much probing and testing. Such probing and testing is done within the immediate surrounding, family, school and society. Past experiences of acceptance or lack of acceptance, and present experiences of opportunity to probe and test are very important aspects in the search for identity.

The negative dimension (or the danger) of this period is the possibility of identity diffusion. Despite the seeming rebelliousness against any form of authority, the young person is usually very sensitive to what adults think of him/her. This is particularly true when the adult world brands a youngster as "delinquent". There is a good chance that the youngster will oblige the adult world by being a delinquent. Unable to identify with the world of children and not accepted in the world of adults, the peer-group is often a natural direction for the adolescent. The formation of "gangs" is not a surprising phenomenon.

It is interesting to observe how an adolescent can run away from the discipline at home and submit to a much more rigorous discipline of a gang or peer-group. It would seem that this form of "independence" tells us that the adolescent does not necessarily reject authority, but asks for personal recognition. Important changes are caused by the three major aspects which I mentioned before, physical appearance, new personality relationships, and personal independence. If these changes are not met adequately there is a danger that the identity of the young person will be diffused. This means it stays in a condition of groping and searching.

Since the earlier stages of development have already influenced the sense of personal value, it is obvious that there is a close relationship with the previous stages. This is particularly true since frequently the same accepting or suppressing surrounding tries to guide the young person through the challenges of this stage. The personal security of the *adults* and *their* ability to accept values different from their own, without compromising true values, is very important. Young people at this stage often want to lean on the personal security of adults.

Intimacy vs. Isolation

The challenge/turmoil of adolescence slowly eases over into the stage of young adulthood which covers approximately the age of eighteen to twenty five. This new period can best be described as the expression and confirmation of the degree of identity which adolescence has brought to the individual. Let us assume that the individual has found a solid degree of personal identity. In such favorable circumstances it can be expected that he/she feels a deep sense of personal value and security. This sense of value and security is not merely a personal possession which is to be guarded. It is rather a personal dimension which is to be manifested and shared with others without suffering a personal loss.

Intimacy as it is understood in this present context is primarily the tendency and the ability to allow oneself to be known deeply by others. It does not mean the urge to pour out one's inner guts for anyone who wants to listen. On the contrary, true intimacy contains a degree of cautiousness. True intimacy is the ability to reveal one's inner self to others when this is constructive and beneficial for oneself and the other. True intimacy is based upon a sense of personal value and is utilized as a constructive contribution to one's own development as well as to the development of others.

The sense of personal value is most intimately related to one's self-image as man or as woman. It includes consciously or unconsciously the mutually complementary dimensions of masculinity and femininity. The deep man-woman relationships, therefore, are to appear at this age level. Earlier existing relationships are not discontinued, but in the developing awareness of personal identity they receive new depths and new dimensions.

The opposite pole which contributes to the tension and balance is isolation. The ground of isolation is the inner awareness or feeling of personal lack of value. There is a doubt about one's meaningfulness to others. It is a normal human need to cover up this doubt of personal meaningfulness either by withholding intimate self-communication, or by constantly drawing the attention of others to some other and less threatening areas of one's personality. Withholding intimate communication can often be expressed in boisterousness or in placing oneself at the center of a peer-group by superficial activities.

Obviously, there is no pure expression of unreserved intimacy or of total isolation. In normal circumstances there is a certain balance in which each individual feels his/her way into the emotional life of other persons. It is a constant effort to find out to what extent one is acceptable and to what extent one can accept the personality of the other. This period of intimacy vs. isolation is in normal circumstances the period in which the personality ripens toward the ability of an intense (and permanent) commitment to another person or to an ideal.

Generativity vs. Stagnation or Self-absorption

It is almost impossible to indicate a transition, or even a real difference between this stage of development and the previous one. This stage of generativity vs. stagnation refers to full adulthood and covers the period of approximately the age between twenty five and forty. In a sense it is the fulfillment of the previous stage. The urge and ability for true intimacy has come to a concrete (mature) expression. It has grown into a self-giving through which the individual contributes to the depth and meaningfulness of one or more other persons, and in which the individual has deepened his/her own personality.

In the usual man-woman relationships it has led to a conjugal relationship and the often therewith connected parenthood. In such circumstances it means literally the generation of new life. Generativity is, however, much wider than physical procreation. It includes the self-expression in every constructive relationship. It takes place between partners in marriage, between friends of the same and/or different sexes. It is a dimension of celibate love and celibate relationship which constructively contributes to the development of other personalities and to the conveyance of deep spiritual values. Generativity is the constructive self-communication of the personality in all its different forms.

The courage of creative self-giving is always limited to a certain degree because of the experience of personal incompleteness. This is the same fear (hesitation) which we have indicated in earlier stages as a consequence of less favorable experiences. The presence of such hesitations means a certain stagnation in self-giving. The constructive and creative power is not fully activated. It is a fear of intimacy, a fear of self-communication, a fear to be rejected if one were really known to the other person.

No person lives in a vacuum, and if there is a fear to

reach out to others then the individual becomes preoccupied with him/herself. Consequently, there is a self-absorption or a concern about one's own acceptability with others. The underlying question in the mind of the individual seems to be (consciously or unconsciously), "How do I come across to others?" instead of "Do I contribute to others?" The concern seems not to be that one's personality is called to contribute positively to others, but that others should contribute to one's own development. Such a person seems unable to give because of the strong need to appropriate, seems to be unable to create because of the need to be created. Here also, there is no pure form of either extreme, but every individual develops a balance between both of them. In this search for a balance, hopefully, he/she finds the creative tension which is the giving and taking of the adult human personality.

Integrity vs. Despair or Disgust

The final stage of development in the structure of the personality is the stage in which all the previous steps towards growth seem to fall into place. The earliest stages leading up to the establishment of an independent and personal identity have brought the individual to a form of adulthood in which he/she was able to express a personal and constructive self-revelation and self-communication. The experience of these dimensions provide a certain tranquility and serenity in which a person is able to give and to receive. It is a giving without imposition, it is a receiving without a feeling of suspicion or threat.

Integrity does not mean the absence of limitations or a blindness for one's own weaknesses. Integrity means the knowledge and the acceptance of one's strengths together with one's weaknesses. Integrity is not a boasting about one's goodness nor a fear for one's limitations, but the acceptance of the "wholeness" that one is. One can accept one's weaknesses without condoning them. One can work for perfection without being paralyzed by the presence of imperfections.

Such an integrity, however relative it may be, is not always achieved. Its absence, to the degree that it is experienced, causes a feeling of despair for not being able to be the person of one's dreams or expectations. It may cause a feeling of disgust because of personal inability to achieve what one feels one ought to have been. It is a form of self-rejection which, because of age and lack of opportunity, does not offer any prospect for improvement. The condition of a person of mature age is usually somewhere between a perfect self-acceptance and a total despair. It may be helpful to remember that the very first stages contain already the potential for later integrity, and that the present form of integrity is a development of the earliest stages of growth. However, the earliest stages have never ceased to exist, and what was underdeveloped in the past is still open to further growth and maturation.

In the study of these eight developmental stages I have tried to stay as close as possible to the meaning of these stages as this is discussed in the various writings of its author, Erik Erikson. Unavoidably, I have also looked at them in the perspective of their meaning and usefulness for this particular study. From a certain point of view this introduces a bias into their understanding. From another point of view, however, the study of these stages in this specific perspective may bring into focus a specific meaning and depth which would otherwise remain in the background.

Again I want to stress that these developmental stages of the human personality are not the source of the other aspects which we want to study in subsequent chapters. I want to stress particularly that they are not the source from which Christian virtues originate. They do, however, provided the form in which these other aspects, including Christian virtues, express themselves in daily human life.

Diagram 1, as shown on the next page, is an effort to visualize the sequence of the stages of psycho-socio development and their mutual interrelatedness.

The center of the diagram is left open to represent the *unstructured source of personality* which influences every stage of growth. Starting at the right top with Basic Trust vs. Basic Mistrust the other stages follow clockwise until the circle closes with Integrity vs. Despair. Each developmental stage flows forth from the previous one and connects with all the other stages in the unstructured center. The other stages are present in each individual stage either as basis or as potential, and all contribute to the development of all. The presence of all in the unstructured source (or center) is meant to indicate the epigenetic nature of the various stages.

Three circles of the diagram are left open to indicate that at this moment we are dealing with only one dimension of the human wholeness. The other aspects are: the criteria for mental health, the ethical modalities, and the virtues. The open circles remind us that we are not studying the psycho-socio crises independently from the other dimensions. We are only taking the first step in a process of development.

I preferred the circular over a linear presentation since a circular presentation indicates more clearly the mutual interdependence than a linear one. However, neither the circular nor the linear presentation is perfect. Each has its own advantages and disadvantages. For clarity sake I will give the linear presentation together with the circular at the end of this book.

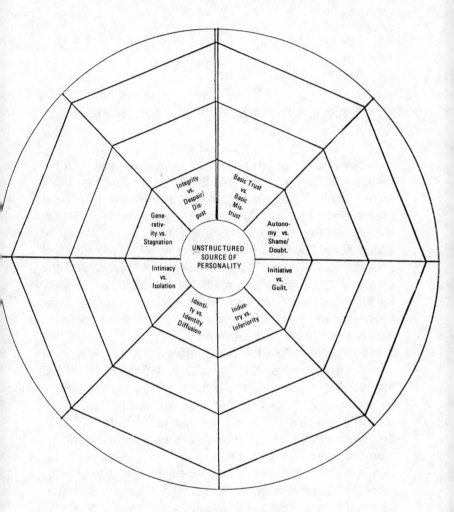

Diagram 1:

Psycho-socio crises in order of development
and mutual interrelatedness

3. BASIC CRITERIA FOR MENTAL HEALTH

The study of the structural developmental stages of the human personality is only one aspect in the understanding of the whole human being. Another, not less important aspect, is the way and the degree of mental health in which the personality expresses itself. Mental health is not an added dimension, it is rather a form of self-expression and behavior in which the individual sees him/herself and the surroundings (human and material) in which he/she lives. Personality structure and mental health are not interchangeable but neither can they be understood independently from each other.

Psychologists and other professionals in behavioral sciences are very reluctant to give a definition of mental health. They rather point to certain criteria which ought to be present to a degree before a person can be considered mentally healthy. Ethicists and spiritual leaders also are deeply convinced of the importance of mental health for moral behavior and spiritual growth. The capacity for personal responsibility is an essential requirement for moral behavior. They are convinced, too, that intellectual knowledge and emotional stability are not the same as moral goodness or sanctity, and that lack of mental health is not a source of immorality.

Therefore, in our study of the human relationship to God it seems to be essential to have at least a grasp of the basic dimensions or criteria for mental health. However, we want to avoid any judgment concerning the degree of mental health that might be required for religious growth.

The concepts which are used to express the criteria for mental health are dynamic concepts. This means that they not only try to indicate a certain degree of the suggested quality, for example a certain degree of self-acceptance, but also a dynamic tension between the two extremes of this concept. Thus a criterion as "self-acceptance" indicates the balance and the balancing within the individual between the feelings of strong personal acceptability and non-acceptability. Although the basic scale of this balance is more or less given in the personality structure, there are outside influences which continuously change this balance.

The eight criteria for mental health as they are presented in this study have a strong mutual interdependence. There is also a certain sequence from the first to the eighth so that the first seems to be more basic than the last. However, the eighth criterion cannot develop without the first, the first cannot fully develop without the last. With this continuous interaction in mind we see the sequence as follows:

1. Self-acceptance.

   This refers to the degree in which a person is able to recognize his/her own qualities without undue dissatisfaction or shame, and in which the total personality, with good and less good qualities, is experienced as worthwhile.

2. Self-actualization (or self-confidence).

   If self-acceptance views the personality on its own value, self-actualization looks at the personality in its relationship with others. It does not look primarily to the degree in which it is accepted by others, but to the degree in which a person is accepted *in the activation of its potential* or in reaching out to others.

3. Balance of personal values.

Where the first two criteria seem to point in opposite directions, namely, the acceptance of self to one-self, and the acceptance of one-self to others, there is a need to bring these two together into a one-ness of human approach. The balance of personal values is the ability to activate one's capacities toward a personal development as well as toward the constructive development of others.

4. Autonomy.

Autonomy as a criterion for mental health is not to be confused with the concept of autonomy in the second psycho-socio crisis. In the psycho-socio crisis *autonomy* refers to the motor development. As a criterion for mental health, it takes the earlier three stages together and refers to the ability to make decisions with a certain amount of independence, based upon a *set of inner standards* by which one can direct oneself without undue dependence on others and without undue resistance against influences from others.

5. Perception of reality.

The actual self-expression based upon a set of inner values demands an accurate perception of reality. This means the ability to see reality free from emotional distortion, not exclusively through one's own limited vision, but to allow for objective dimensions. Further it demands that one is able to see other persons in their own value and not simply in their value in relation to one's own needs. Finally it is the ability to use tensions positively. Mental health does not mean having no tensions but using tensions constructively.

6. Ability to love.

Love means many things, perhaps mostly the positive self-value which allows a person to offer him/herself to another person, and to accept the self-offering of the other constructively. Further, love is a commitment to the good of others, and in the good of others one finds one's own growth. All the previous criteria come together in the expression of love. The inability to love means a self-centeredness which prevents the unfolding of the personality.

7. Adequacy in interpersonal relationships.

Constructive interaction with other persons is a very delicate ability. It is the most fundamental requisite for love and for personal growth. An adequacy in interpersonal relationships demands that an individual has a reasonable amount of aggressiveness when occasions demand it. At the same time such an individual would not allow him/herself to be dominated. Nor would he/she try to dominate others or to push them around. Adequacy in interpersonal relationship is very important in the development of love; at the same time it is developed and strengthened through love.

8. Efficiency in meeting situations.

Human life is a continuous challenge which constantly demands readjustment. The ability to adapt behavior to the efficient utilization of unexpected circumstances presupposes sufficient knowledge of one's own abilities, and sufficient flexibility to re-direct them. Efficiency in meeting situations implies that the individual is not limited to one stereotyped manner of acting, yet can remain his/her own self throughout adaptation. It also implies that the surrounding is not considered as unchangeable but that both auto-plastic (personal) as well as allo-plastic (environment) changes and modifications are possible.

It would be possible to give more or more detailed criteria for mental health. These eight have been selected because they seem to constitute a certain continuum. Each successive criterion presupposes the earlier criteria while simultaneously each subsequent criterion contributes to the development and growth of the previous ones. Thus there seems to be an interaction which is quite similar to the interaction which exists between the psycho-socio crises which we have studied in the previous chapter.

There also seems to be a strong interrelation between the eight criteria for mental health as they are presented here and the psycho-socio crises. In the following pages I will make an effort to show how the criteria for mental health and the psycho-socio crises in the sequence in which they are presented have an interrelationship. It is not my intention to prove that self-acceptance flows forth from basic trust or basic mistrust, or vice versa. Obviously, self-acceptance is much more visible and explicit in the mature integrated person than in the infant. Yet, the form of self-acceptance seems to be closely related to the early experiences in which the infant felt accepted or not accepted for its own value. The degree of self-acceptance corresponds largely to the balance between trust and mistrust. The various aspects of this intertwining are important for the understanding of the human wholeness. We will study each individual criterion for mental health in relation to the various stages of the psycho-socio development.

Self-acceptance

Self-acceptance is a concept which escapes accurate definition. It is a dynamic concept which is subject to constant influences from within the personality as well as from without. Perhaps it can be described as the experiential vision of oneself. This experiential vision is partly a conscious awareness and partly an attitude which is there and which has a strong influence but which is not dependent on knowledge and/or intellectual insight.

Self-acceptance has two major sources, namely, the vision of or the experience of one's own personal qualities, and the understanding of one's acceptability by others, particularly by important persons in one's life. These two sources are inseparably connected and both are subject to deeper understanding and to continuous change in different circumstances. Consequently, self-acceptance cannot be related to a particular stage of development exclusively. It relates to any stage of development and is an important element in every form of growth.

However, since the basic attitude of self-value finds its origin in the earliest human experience, the form of self-acceptance seems to be more closely related to the earliest developmental stage. In the earliest human experiences the infant feels whether it is accepted and loved for its own sake and value or for the sake of others, or whether perhaps it is only tolerated. Accordingly, though at this stage totally unconsciously, it begins to accept itself as a personal value or as a utilitarian object, or perhaps even as an unwanted burden.

In the previous chapter we have tried to indicate how this earliest balance between basic trust and basic mistrust in the human community influences every subsequent stage of development. This influence takes place mostly through the self-acceptance or self-image which is produced by this balance. Every stage of development is a form of self-expression, but self-expression is closely related to the self-image which the individual wants to manifest or to hide.

For this reason I am inclined to find the root for self-acceptance in the psycho-socio stage of basic trust vs. basic mistrust. From this original root it continues to influence the development of the whole personality, particularly the form and the degree of mental health in the individual. The person who sees him/herself as having "no value" can hardly be expected to develop constructive interhuman relationships. The person who sees him/herself as the center of the universe is apt to see every other person as an object that might serve his/her purpose for self-fulfillment. Either of the extremes or any balance between them has its specific influence upon the intellectual and emotional development or expression of a person.

Self-actualization (or self-confidence)

The human being is by nature dynamic, this means that the human qualities must be developed and that this development is more than a biological growth process. This developmental process demands a personal involvement as well as an openness to outside influences.

Personal involvement has various aspects. It not only means the activation of one's capacities, but also the vision of one's acceptability by others. Further, it is very important to know to what degree one is at ease with oneself. Where there is a low degree of self-acceptance the acceptability by others-particularly by important persons in one's life has a much deeper meaning.

These two major aspects, the degree of self-confidence and the degree of being accepted by others, play a significant role at any stage of development. They influence strongly the constructive dimension of human self-expression. Consequently, they have also their influence on the degree of mental health in the individual. The person with a poor self-image, afraid not to be accepted by others, will be much more subject to fear and insecurity than a person who is self-confident and who feels accepted by others.

Despite the fact that self-actualization and self-confidence are essential at every stage of development, it would seem that they are more clearly shaped by the psychological/emotional influences during the period which is the psycho-socio stage of autonomy. This psycho-socio crisis of autonomy refers primarily to personal self-realization in motor development and its acceptability by others. However, the mentality or attitude which is developed during this stage will contribute largely to the form in which later self-expression will take place. This stage has its influence simultaneously a) on the vision of one's personal value; b) on the acceptability of one's self-expression by others; c) on the vision of the power to control others by one's personal qualities or activities.

During this early period of life these three influences are present but unconscious. Later in life these same influences continue to exercise their pressure or direction on the human self-activation. In order to grasp the form and the extent of this direction and pressure it is important to see it at its root, i.e. in relation to the second stage of psycho-socio development.

Balance of Personal Values

The first two criteria for mental health which we described briefly above deal with opposite directions. Self-acceptance contains a form of introversion in which the major concern is the value of one's own personality. Self-actualization is more an expression of extroversion with a concern for one's relationship to others. Although neither of them is totally one-directional and both overlap to a certain extent, the full functioning of both needs an intellectual and emotional capacity to bring both directions together into one orientation of the whole personality.

It would be possible to describe the balance of personal values as a process in which the goal-directedness of the internal drives and the demands of the external reality become integrated. Without such a process the individual's approach to life would become quite distorted. Either he/she would stay within one's own self-concept and have a very unrealistic approach to life, or there would be such a preoccupation with external facts that the personality development would be totally based upon external demands with little or no concern for internal qualities. The balance of personal values tries to avoid these extremes.

Obviously, the need for this balance makes itself felt at every stage of development. We might even say that the more mature a person is the more accurate will be the balance between the internal and external demands. However, when we try to discover the more evident origin of this balance we must go back to early stages of childhood. It would seem that the third stage of psycho-socio development, initiative vs. guilt, provides the shape and the form in which this balance between internal and external demands presents itself.

In the stage of initiative vs. guilt the child lives largely in its own fantasy which expresses itself in play. The child, however, perceives this fantasy and play as a reality, as a real expression of him/herself. It is the earliest effort to bring the internal self-value and the external acceptability into an harmonious expression. This early expression might be very limited, but it remains nonetheless for the child the first test of the value of the whole personality. If it succeeds it can continue to express itself, if it fails the "self" will be perceived as of little value. Not only will this self-perception show a lack of value, it will also contain a feeling of personal blame for the failure. This blame becomes a feeling of guilt connected with the constitution of the personality itself.

The balance between these two extreme possibilities is

the mental/emotional condition in which the individual will approach life. The balance which is achieved at this stage of life is the shape in which the internal and external demands begin to be integrated. The degree and form of integration will also have a strong impact upon the mental health of the individual.

Autonomy, or the ability to act on a set of inner values

In its usual meaning the word *autonomy* suggests the condition of being one's own master, making one's own decisions and giving personally a direction to one's way of life. It is in a certain sense the implicit or explicit goal of every human being to be autonomous. Autonomy is closely related to a sense of personal value and freedom. It gives a sense of personal dignity.

Autonomy is also a very difficult concept to understand. A human being is by nature related to other persons and needs other persons. The relationship with others is a necessary element for personal growth. This necessary relationship with others means also a *dependence* on others, therefore, autonomy is not the same as total independence. True autonomy accepts the need and the reality of dependence on other persons.

Dependence on other persons does not exclude the development of personal qualities. The opposite is true. Personal qualities ought to develop (and can only develop) in interchange with other persons. Real growth must have sufficient independence to develop personal qualities, and must accept sufficient dependence to allow influences from others. Consequently, one can show a lack of autonomy by overly relying on the influence of others or by unreasonably rejecting influences from others. To reject totally any outside influence may be authocratic but not autonomous.

From a certain point of view autonomy is an adult

quality. This means it can have its full development only in adulthood. It is obvious, however, that its development started much earlier. We may say that the most primitive form of autonomy is already encountered in the first stage of psycho-socio development where basic trust and basic mistrust search for a balance, though totally unconsciously. Real autonomy demands an intellectual and emotional awareness of what one is doing. At least it is necessary to be aware of the underlying values of one's approach to life. One must be able to recognize the reason for one's activities.

The appreciation of values is both experience and learning. To appreciate the value of one's personal activity a person needs the experience that one's activities are acceptable or rejectable to others, and it is necessary to know why the activities are accepted or rejected. The earliest stage of life in which such experience and such knowledge seem to be both present is the school age. It is the age of industry vs. inferiority, this means the stage in life in which the youngster wants to test his/her acceptability through activity.

When personal initiative and self-activation are accepted there is the beginning of a conscious personal value. Where such acceptance is lacking the appreciation of one's personal value remains low. When the young person's initiative is inacceptable, it is most likely that the individual will become quite dependent on others in order to please them, or he/she might become quite rebellious in order to create a feeling of personal value. Both expressions manifest a lack of autonomy. It would seem that the balance which is developed at this stage is quite important for the form of future approach to life.

True autonomy is also able to recognize threats against

oneself and to mobilize the forces to counteract the threats. Autonomy helps to develop one's own worldview and act upon it.

Perception of reality

There is no doubt that reality exists independent from the individual who perceives it. The reality is the world outside the person. It is the surrounding within which the individual acts and reacts. It is one of the major influences in the formation of the personality. This reality, existing independently from the individual, is never perceived independent from the individual. The outside reality is by necessity a relation to the individual who perceives it. Consequently, the position or the condition of the perceiver adds a special dimension to the reality which does not properly belong to the object itself but which is peculiar to the perceiver.

The more a person is preoccupied with his/her own personality the more a subjective element will enter into the perception of the object. The tendency of the personality will strongly influence the meaning of the object which is perceived. One person can look at a modern housing complex and see nothing else but its commercial value. Another person will see primarily its practical aspects as living quarters. Both these views are quite subjective, but they can be quite healthy at the same time and based upon much objective reality.

In other circumstances objectivity can be thwarted. One person may view a certain authority as a valuable assistance in the search for the unfolding of one's personal qualities. This same authority may mean to another person a severe threat to personal development. For a third person the same authority may be an indispensable support for any decision making. In the three instances the reality of 'authority' is perceived in very different ways, despite the fact that it is the same authority.

If we assume that this particular authority is quite reasonable, then only the perception of the first person can be considered objective and real. The other two are dealing more with their own fears than with reality. Their own personality structure prevents their seeing the external conditions. Thus the perception of reality is a very important aspect in the mental health of an individual.

Earlier stages of growth have contributed greatly to the manner in which reality is perceived. The importance of this manner of perception reaches through all the forms and degrees of development. At the early stages of development it is more an instinctive feeling. Here we are dealing with a grasping which is strongly influenced by a conscious perception of the outside. This means we are focusing more explicitly upon the interaction between the understanding of oneself and of the outside. It presupposes an experience of both which has already provided the individual with a certain form of identity in this world.

The acquired form of identity is put to a very severe test during the period of adolescence. Physically, intellectually and emotionally the individual seems to be thrown off balance. Because of the new dimensions of physical and relational existence it becomes for the young person quite difficult to see reality as it is. There is the very real possibility of developing a very "subjective" vision of reality which will form the basis for a later approach to life. If the adolescent is not understood and respected, future attitudes may become quite negative. Negative attitudes experienced in earlier life have a strong influence upon what happens in adolescence. However, the manner in which reality is perceived at this time contributes immensely to the vision of the future.

The ability to love

Throughout the earlier stages of development and the corresponding criteria for mental health, it has become clear that interpersonal relationships are an indispensable aspect of healthy human growth. Among the interpersonal relationships love must be considered as the most intimate and the most essential.

Love is not only a romantic feeling, or a pleasurable feeling of well-being. Love means the involvement of a whole personality. Love is a feeling, but then in the sense as described by Charles David: "feeling is a response springing forth from what we are". Love is a response of the whole personality toward another person in which such elements as care, responsibility, respect, and knowledge[2] are activated and direct themselves to the other person.

Love is not simply doing things for another. Love has as its two major components the activation of one's own qualities and the constructive well-being of the other person. If there is no constructive concern for one's own qualities and development, it is easy to fall into a form of enslavement to others. If there is no deep concern for the constructive development of the other persons, the "expressions of love" easily become an imposition.

Love also presupposes that one allows one's own qualities to be known to the other. One can be loved only to the extent that one allows oneself to be known by the other. It is important to express one's self in actions, but actions alone can remain superficial. If a person acts out of love, with a respectful concern for a minority group, this person reveals only a very small part of his/her personality. In a love of friendship, particularly in conjugal love, the self-revelation is much deeper.

It is this kind of love, the love of friendship, which is most important for mental health. It is the ability to be intimate with others, this means, to allow others to know one's deeper and one's personal inclinations. Intimacy demands the kind of self-esteem which allows a person to give oneself to others and to receive from others. Love is not a prerogative of adulthood. Children can love very deeply. Nor is love a prerogative of maturity. Immature persons can and do love in their own ways. However, in the love of the child and of the immature person are elements of need-fulfillment which must be overcome in the process of full human development.

Love does not originate during the period of the psycho-socio crisis of intimacy vs. isolation. But the ability to love is closely related to the ability to be intimate with others. Conversely, in a loving relationship the ability for intimacy increases, while an increased expression of true intimacy can lead to a deeper love.

Adequacy in interpersonal relationships

The ability to love has another dimension which is closely related to it, yet, which at the same time forms a specific quality independent from the ability to love. This quality is the adequacy in interpersonal relationships. In every human being is a necessary tension between the need for self-fulfillment and one's meaningfulness for the society.

Although it is true that human growth is inconceivable without a mutual exchange between the individual and other members of the society, there is always the danger that one individual will try to dominate others. In the expression of personal self-realization it is very easy to infringe upon others, or to be pressured by others.

Effective and constructive interhuman relationships demand a certain degree of adequacy which displays a reasonable aggressiveness. This adequacy allows a person to push him/herself when the occasion demands it, but at the same time it prevents a person from dominating others.

This balance between sufficient self-assertiveness and acceptance of the individuality of others is only possible in a person who is secure in him/herself. Moreover, this balance is only possible when a person is not only convinced of his/her own value in the development and growth of others, but also of the value of others for their own growth and development. It is the attitude of a person who, in the true sense of the word, is creative. The adequacy in interpersonal relationships means a creativity with regard to one's own personality as well as with regard to the personality of others.

It would seem, therefore, that although adequacy in interpersonal relationships is a very relative concept, it is very closely related to the creative self-giving and the creative receiving of the personality. Although it belongs to every stage of development in the human personality, it has a particular relationship with the stage of generativity in human development. This same adequacy is quite significant in the process of mental health. One of the first signs of problems with mental/emotional health is the loss of ability to live with other persons. Obviously, not everyone can live with anyone. Some personalities are almost natural opposites. However, the inability to live with anyone, or the loss of ability to live with persons with whom one used to live in friendship, asks for serious consideration of the direction of development.

Efficiency in meeting situations

Challenges of life occur at any age level and at any stage of development. There are always situations which could not be foreseen and which demand a new arrangement of capacities and activation of potential. During the earlier stages of life such unforeseen circumstances can become easily upsetting and disturbing, particularly since they are often circumstances in which one has no experience. Lack of experience means that one is not yet familiar with one's own abilities and with the possible reactions of other persons.

At a more mature age there is a better ability of tackling new situations. One has experienced one's own abilities and one's acceptability with others. One has found a balance between one's personal value and one's meaningfulness for other persons. A sufficient personal security makes it possible to adapt to others without being threatened with loss of dignity. Past experiences can be invaluable in weighing the various aspects of situations, and thus lead to solutions of problems which at earlier age-lebels may have looked almost insurmountable.

Efficiency in meeting situations is not by itself a sign or guarantee of mental health. It can be an expression of a highly calculated approach to life while there is a deep personal insecurity. However, if we are dealing with a person who does not have to prove him/herself, but who has a constructive concern for others, then this ability to deal with new situations becomes a balanced and mature expression of internal strength. It becomes an expression of personal health and a source of a constructive contribution to the human society. It is the meeting place of all the strengths of the personality, and thus it is in a special manner related to the mature age level.

In summarizing this interaction we may say that a

healthy person lives on a personal value level which is meaningful not only for him/herself but also for other persons. A mentally heatlhy person lives in a personal security which is not threatened by normal influences from others, on the contrary, it is strengthened by contributions from the outside. In such persons there is a contentment with oneself and an adaptability to others.

In the approach to daily life, every human being, whatever the degree of health and balance may be, gives a certain indication of what sort of behavior is beneficial and/or acceptable. These different visions on acceptability and non-acceptability of behavioral approaches are the subject of the next chapter.

Diagram 2 tries to visualize how the criteria for mental health interconnect by placing them within the confines of a circle. In a sense all are equally important, each criterion contributes to the completeness of the other criteria. At the same time the diagram wants to indicate how the criteria for mental health relate to the developmental stages of the human personality. The criteria form a circle around the stages of personality development to suggest that they need the personality as their basis. In the diagram, as it is presented here, the criteria for mental health are related to the stages of personality development from which they draw their basic form. The relationship of each and all criteria to each and every stage of personality development is indicated through their common ground in the unstructured source of the personality. If the two circles would be independent so that the stages of personality development could turn and correspond to any other stage of the criteria for mental health one would see that each stage has a relationship with each stage of the other group.

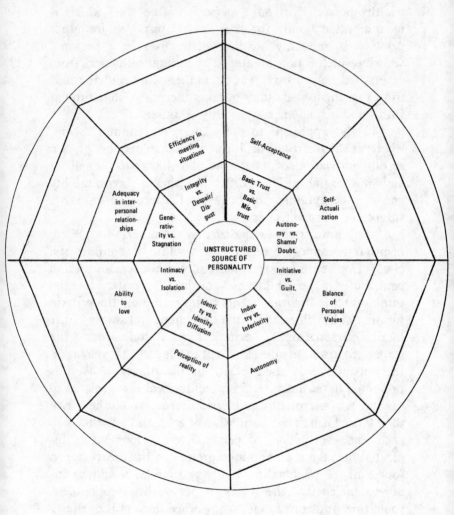

Diagram 2:

Criteria for Mental Health in mutual interdependence and in their
relationship to psycho-socio crises

4. ETHICAL MODALITIES AND
THE STRUCTURE OF THE HUMAN PERSONALITY

Conscious human self-expression has necessarily an ethical value. However imperceptible an individual contribution may be, every individual human activity has some impact upon the individual as well as upon other persons who are connected with the activity. This means that there is no such thing as an indifferent human action. Material objects and situations, considered independently from human involvement, can be considered as indifferent, but as soon as they are the result of a human activity they share in the ethical value of the action itself. For example, human beings die. This happening in itself has no moral value, but as soon as a human being is involved in the cause of this death, we enter the field of morality.

We can take a less drastic example. Human beings stumble when they walk along uneven paths. This stumbling in itself has no moral or ethical value. If, however, another human being is causing this person to stumble, then we enter again the field of morality, although in a much less serious degree than in the former example. Conversely, if a person stumbles, for whatever reason, and another person can just in time prevent this person from hurting, then we enter also into the field of morality. Causing to stumble and preventing it are both human self-expressions which have a moral value (or fall under an ethical evaluation). True moral evaluation depends on the interaction of the material importance of the result, its impact upon other persons and the depth of personal involvement.

One may wonder legitimately why this question concerning possibility of indifferent human actions is mentioned in a study on the integration of human values. The reason is that I want to emphasize that morality is not simply a matter of objective rules. Morality (moral value or ethical value) has a very deep personal foundation. The personal involvement of the individual is an essential aspect in moral evaluation. Personal involvement, however, is not always a matter of free will or of deliberate choice. Many decisions which are made by an individual are strongly influenced by the structure of the personality.

In many instances the personal decision (or choice) of the individual is so inextricably interwoven with the personality structure that the action receives a specific personal flavor different from the action of any other person. Seemingly identical activities in identical circumstances may have a very different moral value. An example of this is found in St. Paul's letter to the Corinthians in which he describes two kinds of people who ate meat consecrated to the gods. One kind of persons were convinced that idols did not exist at all so that the consecration of the meat was meaningless. The other kind of persons (because of their education) were internally not so sure and violated their conscience by eating this meat (I Cor. 8:1-13).

This example deals with the structure of the personalities, not simply with rules or with making a choice. The personality structure has a great influence upon the morality of human activities. Human activities, as expressions of the personality, belong to the integration of human values. The moral value of the activities is not determined by the personality structure, but the structure of the personality has a direct influence upon the morality of the actions. We see this in the example of St. Paul's letter to the Corinthians.

For this reason I find it necessary to spend some time to study the specific qualities of the personality in so far as they influence the moral value of human actions. A personality structure itself is never good or bad. It is only in its activation and in its relational expression toward others that it influences the value of the actions. In the personality structure there is a basic structure or attitude in which self-expression and values are approached. This basic structure and attitude provides an inclination or predisposition which contributes to the direction for ethical evaluation. These inclinations and predispositions form as it were *ethical modalities* which are a dimension of the personality and which co-determine the moral value which a person gives to his/her activities.

These ethical modalities, as I like to call them for lack of a better name, are presented only as modalities, i.e., forms for evaluation. This means that I want to refrain very carefully from any moral evaluation at this point. I want only to study the personality and its ways in which it expresses itself and relates to God. In the human relationship to God these ethical modalities not only influence moral evaluations but also the development of virtues. Consequently, they belong to the structure of human wholeness and human integration.

In the development of these ethical modalities I have been inspired by the studies of Lawrence Kohlberg[1] and Jean Piaget.[2] However, since I am less concerned with any degree of guilt or of responsibility the present study is largely a result of personal reflection. It tries to understand the personality pattern rather than the stage of moral development. The presentation of eight ethical modalities is to an extent a random choice. Many further refinements can be made. In the perspective of this study and in an effort to understand the whole human integration in the light of a known study of personality development, I decided to take only eight modalities. Individually these modalities can be related to the developmental stages of the personality, and as a group they form a completeness by themselves. Each ethical modality is to a certain extent contained in all the others and all modalities contribute to the full development of each individual modality. Yet, individually and successively they are related to the successive stage of development.

First I will present the ethical modalities in progressive development. In the presentation itself I try to indicate two extremes. This is not to indicate that the real balanced modality lies somewhere in between, but to suggest a creative tension. Every human action has certain aspects that favor its performance and it has other aspects that seem to disadvise it. The tension between these two belongs to the human approach to life.

Source of values from within vs. Source of values from without
The basic element and source for evaluation is the source of the values themselves. When a personality can find values within itself the approach to life is very different from the personality whose values are totally dependent on outside acceptability. A person who is totally dependent on outside acceptability will often lack continuity and conviction.

Willing cooperation vs. forced submission
When cooperating with others is a matter which is almost connatural, in that there is room for a smooth development of the personality. An individual develops a very different approach to life when

cooperation is demanded by fear. The person with "inner" values can usually cooperate more freely than a person who is totally dependent on outside acceptance.

Accepting personal responsibility vs. sense of self-rejection

It is not difficult for an individual to assume personal responsibility when a value comes from within and when there can be a free cooperation. If the value is imposed and forced upon the individual, there will be an avoiding of responsibility and a feeling of personal worthlessness.

Searching for personal insight vs. imposition of commandments

For an action to be human in the full sense of the word, and for a person to assume responsibility for it, there must be a certain degree of knowledge. Here again, based upon the the stages of earlier development, the individual can either be concerned about developing this knowledge in a personal manner, or he/she can rely mostly on the commands which others impose. The imposition of such commandments is usually experienced as an outside influence containing a degree of lack of esteem for the personality and creating an attitude of rebellion or indifference.

Personal acceptability vs. need to prove oneself

It is very important for a person to have a good self-image and to know that one is accepted by others. No normal human being enjoys the sense of being useless to oneself or to others. An individual with a sense of personal value will find it easy to reach out to others. However, when there is a sense of personal uselessness then the individual will very likely be concerned to prove him/herself through activities. Such actions are usually not performed as a contribution to others but as an effort to subject others to oneself.

An openness to sharing vs. a fearful guarding

This modality is an almost necessary consequence of

the previous one. A genuine sense of inner value is a pride to share with others. Such person can allow him/herself to be known to others and can display an openness to others. The absence of a sense of personal value tends to close the personality and makes one guard fearfully what one seems to have. Contributing to others is experienced as a loss and receiving from others is seen as a personal threat.

Source of self-expression vs. narrow self-concern

The sense of worthwhileness of the personality shares in the dynamic nature of the human being. The inner source of value is translated into action. Such action produces not only personal benefits but also contributes to society. Consequently, the sense of personal value which allows an individual to be a source of self-expression enters very deeply into the field of ethical evaluation. The opposite dimension is the preoccupation with one's own good. An almost congenital self-preoccupation becomes a modality of self-expression which colors the value of one's activity.

Integrative self-determination vs. incarceration in commandments

This last modality is similar to the accruement of the earlier forms of development. There remains always a degree of weighing and searching, but past experiences can provide an ease of acting and of assuming responsibility, or they can do the opposite and confirm the personality as a fugitive hiding behind the directions of others. Whatever the balance between these two may be, it colors the human response to one's fellowman and to God.

These ethical modalities are not independent qualities in any individual. They merely are ways and degrees in which an individual grasps the acceptability or inacceptability of his/her activities.

In the beginning of this chapter I mentioned that the structure of the personality has a strong influence upon the way in which a person evaluates the moral acceptability or inacceptability of his/her approach to life. Consequently, it is my strong belief that ethical modalities can be fully understood only in the perspective of the psycho-socio-crises and of the criteria for mental health.

In this comparative study, however, we must be aware of certain differences. The various stages of development in the psycho-socio crises, however intimately they may be intertwined and however they may overlap, show a certain progressive development. The same progressive development can be noticed in the study of the criteria for mental health. The study of the ethical modalities gives a slightly different picture. In these eight stages we do not see primarily a progressive development but rather a succession of concentric circles which cover an ever widening field of human consciousness and self-activation. One person observed, it is as if you throw a stone into the water. The ripples become wider and wider until they cover the width of the stream.

This perspective must remain with us when we study the ethical modalities in the perspective of psycho-socio crises and of criteria for mental health. Each ethical modality extends itself from the most elementary form of development to the most mature form of self-realization. However, since certain ethical modalities are, if we may use the comparison, closer to the center of the concentric circles, their origin and shape may be more related to the earlier stages of development. Just as the later stages of development seem to be based upon earlier stages, so also seem the wider concentric circles to flow forth from the smaller, more concentrated ones.

In this context we can again focus on each individual

ethical modality in order to reflect on it in the light of the stages of personality development and of the criteria for mental health.

Source of values from within vs. Source of values from without

Earlier in this book we have accepted that the most elementary stage of personality development deals with the tension between a basic trust versus a basic mistrust. The basic concept of this tension relates to the manner in which a person experiences acceptance or non-acceptance on his/her own value by the important persons in his/her life.

Based upon this earliest experience the person develops an attitude which forms the ground for future self-acceptance or of self-rejection. The self-accepting person has experienced a value within his/her own personality. Such a person can reach out to others with confidence. This means such a person can present him/herself to others as a person of value who does not fear to be rejected, nor is there a fear to be harmed by the influence of others.

The person who has a low degree of self-acceptance is in a very different situation. The earliest experience of lack of personal value prevents a constructive reaching out to others. Where there is no inner experience of value which can be offered to others, there can hardly be an openness to values which are offered by others. There will be an almost constituent fear that any other influence will cause harm or pain. The basic value will be the degree of acceptability by others with the consequent need to act according to what others may expect.

The concept of basic trust versus mistrust and the degree of self-acceptance are inextricably intertwined. Whenever a person has experienced real or imagined rejection by others the degree of self-value decreases unvoidably. By necessary consequence, the future approaches of other persons will be received in this basic disposition of "being rejected". This means they will be received with suspicion which acts as a protective shield around the personality. Such basic prejudice prevents one seeing the goodness of an action until it has proven its value in this specific instance and for this specific person.

There is a basic need of every human being to deepen and to experience one's own value either by offering oneself to others, by receiving from others, or by mutual exchange. The person "without a feeling of personal value" can hardly offer anything to another person. In reaching out such a person will be more inclined either to impose him/herself upon the other so as to get the external appearance of being important, or to become possessive in order to enhance his/her own value through appropriating the value of the other.

It would seem obvious that the source through which a person experiences his/her personal value has a great influence upon the manner in which goodness or evil is perceived. In the two extremes a person is inclined to see primarily either goodness or evil. According to the balance of the personality structure a person will lean toward one side or the other. Without attributing to this inclination a specific moral value, it would seem that the learned attitude disposes a person toward a specific form of evaluation. This evaluation does not only concern the action of others but also, and perhaps primarily, his/her personal activities. Just as the personality structure and the concept of mental health center around the degree of basic trust and self-acceptance, so also does the ethical inclination center around the source from which the individual seems to perceive all personal values. These three dimensions are closely interrelated.

Willing cooperation vs. Forced submission

Human life cannot be lived without interaction with other persons. This interaction always includes a form of cooperation whether this cooperation is intended or not. Living and working with others is a certain form of adaptation, whether one adapts oneself to the other or makes the other adapt to oneself or whether it is a mutual effort to find a compromise, it is always an adaptive interaction. It will cause a very different feeling in the individual when this interaction is a free choice rather than an imposition.

In order that such interaction may become a free choice it is first of all necessary that a person has been able to develop a basic trust in humanity and that there is a sense of self-acceptance. These basic attitudes have been discussed in the previous pages. It is also necessary that the individual has had the opportunity for self-expression. Unless an individual has experienced the freedom to use his/her qualities with personal initiative, he/she will have been unable to develop a sense of cooperation. He/she may have learned to submit and to adapt, but not to contribute anything to the activity. Cooperation includes a personal contribution to the content, form and execution of the activity.

The ability to contribute cooperatively demands a basic attitude of trust and self-acceptance, which originates in the first stage of the psycho-socio crises. This basic attitude becomes more refined and more precise in the developmental stage of autonomy versus shame. This stage deals with the experience of self-activation. In this stage a person tries the effectiveness of his/her own abilities and experiences their acceptability by others. This experience is more than the activation of abilities. It is a real *self*-activation, so that the acceptance of the activities means the acceptance of the person, while the rejection of the activities is felt as a personal rejection. This personal rejection creates a feeling of shame and doubt which touches the personality itself.

The degree, real or imagined, in which one's activity is accepted by others will also determine the degree of self-confidence. The more acceptable an activity has proved to be, the more one can act with confidence in that particular aspect and in that particular group of people. Whenever actions have proved to be unacceptable the reaction can differ from passive submission to tenacious resistance. Both reactions, though opposites, are forms of self-preservation. They express how this person in these circumstances can experience and maintain a sense of personal dignity and value.

This same deeply personal experience of dignity and value will also color the sense of what is desirable or undesirable in internal and external relationships. Even before there is a personal application or commitment to an action, there is a sense of desirability or undesirability. Obviously, this has no moral dimensions as yet, but this inclination sets the stage for a personal application which is very other-directed or very self-directed, with any in-between shades.

In this application of self, morality enters into the field. Morality is the responsible and evaluative relationship of the self-realizing individual toward the outside world of persons and of material objects. The ability to relate constructively is greatly influenced by the personal feeling of being accepted or by the personal need to demand acceptance. The personality itself has a modality which enhances cooperation or makes cooperation more difficult.

Accepting personal responsibility vs. a sense of self-rejection

Human activity includes always a personal attitude of the person who performs the action. Either one feels personally responsible for the activity and its results, or one shrugs off the responsibility and hides behind outside commands or pressures. To feel personally responsible means to appropriate to oneself the reason, the origin and the goal of the activity. To evade responsibility means to attribute any of these three aspects to circumstances or to other persons and to maintain that one was not acting on one's own choice.

In this context we are dealing with the balance of the internal self-assessment of the individual and the individual's relationship to the outside. It is the balance as to whether the source and value of the activity originates from within the person or from the external circumstances, at least in the opinion of the person who acts. Whenever an agent accepts a personal (internal) reason, goal and origin of an activity, then the agent puts him/herself into the action, i.e., one's personal value is involved and one accepts responsibility. At the other extreme of the scale is the person who acts totally under outside influences and who has a mechanical rather than a personal relationship to the action. Such a person hardly accepts personal responsibility. The internal value of a person and the external performance seem to be different realities.

The balance between the internal and the external value-dimensions creates a certain modality in the person which influences his/her feelings about the acceptability or unacceptability of an action. Consequently, this balance constitutes an ethical modality. This modality is very closely related to the developmental stage which Erik Erikson calls initiative vs. guilt.

In an earlier chapter I have tried to show how at this stage the internal value of a person and the external ability of motor functioning lead to an activity which involves the person as a whole. In the extreme opposites either a person (in and through his/her activity) is accepted and experiences a value, or a person may feel rejected and experiences a feeling of unworthiness which touches the personality itself. It is a personality-unworthiness which is a feeling of being guilty for being what one is. In normal circumstances the blending of the internal value and the external functioning creates a balance in which both responsibility and caution intermingle in the same activity.

The balance of personal values, which I indicated as the mental health criterion which corresponds closest to the stage of initiative vs. guilt, helps us to shed light on this ethical modality. This balance of personal values tries to grasp the vision which the individual wants to realize according to his/her own value and ability and according to the expectations of the surroundings. The acceptability or unacceptability of activities is greatly influenced by this vision of the individual. However, this vision includes a strongly subjective element which creates an inclination toward activities before any aspect of moral evaluation can enter.

This ethical modality of accepting personal responsibility versus a sense of self-rejection indicates the tension between internal and external values. This tension is present at every stage of life and development. However, the form in which it presents itself is closely related to the stage of initiative versus guilt and of the balance of personal values. The ethical direction will become more explicit according to the degree of personal self-acceptance and of the goal directedness of life.

Searching for personal insight vs. imposition of commandments

Personal responsibility requires a certain degree of knowledge about the purpose and/or possible consequences of the action. Without such knowledge an action can be a mechanical performance, but it can hardly be considered a human action. (Sometimes an agent can be held responsible for not developing the required knowledge.) The extent of knowledge required in any human activity is largely determined by the impact which the action might have upon other persons or upon the physical surroundings. For example, when an action involves the preservation of human life, it demands a much deeper knowledge of all circumstances than when it simply concerns a material object of minor value.

Together with the actual (external) dimension of the extent of required knowledge there is also an internal or subjective dimension with regard to knowledge. There is in the agent a certain disposition through which he/she is inclined to search for a personal knowledge before assuming responsibility. This inclination can have many different degrees. In some persons it is a strong need to know the details and the impact of an action before engaging oneself. In other persons there seems to be an inclination to evade such insights and to rely (almost) entirely on outside influences. Although this inclination or disinclination by itself has no moral determination, it does create a modality according to which a person is more likely to act. We may call this an ethical modality which resides in the person and which develops with the personality.

The personality structure to which this ethical modality seems to relate more closely is the stage of industry versus inferiority. This stage marks in the personality the urge to find acceptance by oneself and by others on account of what one can produce. As a developmental stage it is the period in the young person's life in which the fantasy world becomes insufficient. There is a need to prove to oneself and to others through concrete performance one's own value and acceptability. When this effort is unsuccessful, the individual will most likely develop a sense of personal inferiority or lack of personal value.

The degree of personal value in its relation to productive self-expression has a great influence upon the person's approach to life. If the urge for productive action pays off in the form of acceptance by others and a sense of value for oneself, then there will slowly develop a set of inner values on which the individual can act. It is a sense of autonomy which integrates the internal abilities and the outside demands into one productive action. This action flows forth from the individual who has incorporated the outside demands and has integrated them into an attitude which can accept personal responsibility.

If the urge for productive action does not pay off, the individual tends to develop a sense of personal inferiority. When an individual in this state of mind needs to act, the approach is likely to be somewhere between two extremes. There may be either a total submission to the influences from the outside, or strong resistence to them. In either case the activity is largely determined by the outside influences. The personal involvement in such activities is a self-defensive attitude rather than a realization of one's potential. Extremes do not occur very frequently, the usual balance lies somewhere between them.

It is not my intention to study or to evaluate to what degree a person is responsible to seek personal knowledge and insight or to be open to directives by authorities. My purpose is to show that the personality structure itself provides the shape in which personal responsibility is expressed. Personal self-realization includes necessarily a certain degree of self-protection. Some persons have a stronger need for this self-protection than others. Thus they present a different modality in which ethical values are expressed. However, morality is never independent from the objective demands of constructive human interaction.

The first four ethical modalities discussed so far in this chapter form as it were the basis of the ethical personality. A person's individual understanding of the goodness and acceptability of the action is determined by such factors as: where does this person see the source of values; to what extent is cooperation with others possible; to what degree can this person accept responsibility; and is he/she sufficiently self-confident to search for personal insight? The following stages are rather consequences and modifications both of the manner in which individuals express themselves, and of the impact which their self-expression has upon other persons.

Personal acceptability vs. need to prove oneself

Every human activity contains a large element of self-realization. This self-realization can have very different purposes. In certain instances it may be a self-extension or a reaching out in self-giving in order to share with others of one's own richness. Such self-extension is not an imposition which "wants to make oneself accepted by others". It is rather an offering of oneself for the benefit of the other. In other instances this self-extension can be a response to a personal need to prove one's ability, goodness and value. In such cases it is not primarily the benefit of others which is important but one's personal benefit. The other persons are more the object to fill a personal need in the agent rather than being invited to be partners in personal sharing.

Obviously, even when the other persons are partners the agent benefits by the action, but here it is a mutual enrichment rather than a one-sided concern.

In the usual human approach to life the balance lies somewhere in between the two extremes, and this balance will vary with times and circumstances. In the human action is usually a need-fulfillment and a personal satisfaction combined with the concern for others. Whatever the precise balance may be, the actual approach to life is at the same time a disposition in the agent making a certain action desirable or undesirable. There is a modality in the person which leans toward a specific ethical understanding. This ethical modality will influence the person's approach to life and activity.

This ethical modality or inclination is closely related to the structure of the personality. It would seem that it has a specific relationship with the stage of adolescence which is the tension between identity and identity diffusion. I do not say that this ethical modality is a special characteristic of the adolescent stage or that it originates at this stage. The ethical modality manifests itself in every stage of development. But the tension between personal acceptability and the need to prove oneself follows largely the pattern of the tension between identity and identity diffusion.

The search for identity, i.e., the search for the meaning, the value and the importance of one's life with regard to oneself and to others is at the same time a search for personal acceptability. Whenever a person can accept him/herself as a person of value, the relationship with others receives a positive tone. Most of all, however, the relationship of oneself becomes positive. There will be no further need to search all over the place for a form of self-expression which does not have a backlash. The outside reality which presents itself continuously can be taken for what it is. The individual can face the reality without too much personal preoccupation which blurs the vision. On the other hand, where the vision on one's own identity is on a low level, the vision on reality is confused and the individual may have to act in a specific manner which confirms the person he/she wants to be.

Thus the structure of the personality in so far as it provides a balance for personal identity, and the degree to which the perception of reality is free of distortion produce an inclination toward a specific ethical modality. This inclination becomes a part of the human approach to life and activity and forms a subjective dimension in a future moral evaluation of one's actions. The moral evaluation does not belong to this study. At this moment we are searching to *understand* the personality who responds to God.

Openness to sharing vs. fearful guarding

Active concern for the neighbor is usually seen as one of the highest human values in social relationships as well as in Christian virtues. But healthy concern for the neighbor begins, as the Scriptures indicate, with a concern for oneself, namely, "love your neighbor as yourself".

Love contains two major elements, namely, an active respect for the other person and the form of meaningfulness which the other person has for the lover. Both elements are inseparably connected with the vision which the lover has of him/herself. The person with an internal value can reach out to others without fear of loss of his/her own identity. The person with a poor self-image will try to guard the little he/she seems to have. This personal attitude will determine to what degree a person can be open to share his/her own personality with others, or to what degree there is a need to be on guard. It is a modality of the personality which has an immediate bearing upon the basic Christian command of love for the neighbor. This modality determines largely the manner in which human interaction takes place, and it contributes to the degree of constructiveness of this interaction. For this reason we are dealing with an ethical modality as an aspect of the personality itself.

It is important to recognize the structure of the personality which contributes to this degree of openness or closedness. It would seem that the stage of intimacy versus isolation expresses in the personality this basic openness and closedness. Intimacy, as we have seen, is the basic ability and willingness to let one's own deeper self be known to another person and to share this deeper self with the other. The ability and the willingness to be intimate is a basic requirement for the ability to love another person. Earlier I have mentioned that the psychological ability to love is immediately related to the balance between the ability for intimacy and the need for isolation. Persons who are able to be intimate in the proper sense of the word are inclined to reach out to others. Their reaching out is both offering to the other and receiving from the other. Persons who fear intimacy are inclined to withdraw, or at least not to allow anyone to come close to them. When a person who fears intimacy reaches out to others the immediate purpose is often not to offer of oneself to others, but rather to obtain from others for oneself. Even a high degree of generosity can be largely inspired by the need to be meaningful, even if this effort for meaningfulness is not appreciated by others.

It would seem then that the balance in the tension between ability for intimacy and the need for isolation creates a specific form of personality. According to this balance the person would be able to share with others in a personal giving and receiving or to stay aloof from others in a need for personal protectiveness. Neither of these tendencies has in itself a moral evaluation, but they provide a modality upon which a moral evaluation of interhuman exchange will be based. In his/her response to God a human being acts in a similar way. The quality of the response to God is, therefore, very closely aligned with the structure of the personality, although the response to God does not receive its moral value from the personality structure. We may also be able to see at this moment that a growth in the personality, particularly a growth in the ability for intimacy, will have a direct influence upon the person's ability to respond to God.

Source of self-expression vs. narrow self-concern

In the interhuman exchange the agent is always the center of the ongoing activity, but the manner in which one can be the center varies greatly. In some instances, or rather with certain types of personalities, the action seems to flow forth from the inner dimensions of the agent. In other instances, or with other kinds of personalities, the agent seems to draw almost exclusively on others. The latter are the type of personality whose concern seems to be centered on personal acceptability rather than on enriching self-communication. Everyone has met the person who manages to bring every piece of conversation back to his/her personal or family experiences. With such persons no one else has an opportunity to speak out or to express personal problems.

The above description does not contain an evaluation of the personalities which are involved. It simply points to the reality of different expressions and different ways of approaching life. Such different ways of self-expression indicate different modalities of interhuman relationships, and consequently, they suggest also different ethical modalities. The impact upon the surroundings is very different for each pole of the tension of this modality. When a person is sufficiently mature and open to be the inner source of self-expression, the influence upon others will be very different than when the agent needs to be the almost exclusive recipient of the human interaction.

When the impact upon the surroundings is different, and when the form of self-realization is different, we have at least the basis for a difference in ethical evaluation. This difference is closely related to the structure of the personality. It remains therefore important to see what dimensions of the personality structure seem to contribute to this particular type of modality.

We are dealing with self-expression in relation to others. This self-expression is meant to be a form of self-giving. Therefore, we seem to be dealing with a form of generativity and its counter pole, stagnation or self-absorption. Generativity as one of the psycho-socio crisis refers to the whole personality in so far as it is able and willing to contribute to the growth-process in others and allows others to contribute to its own growth-process. Earlier we have seen that, in more favorable circumstances, the degree of generativity is based upon a healthy basic trust and upon a secure form of identity. The degree of generativity will be considerably lower when basic trust and firm identity are lacking. In such circumstances there will be a stagnation, a lack of inner movement and an absorption with one's own needs.

As a consequence of this personality structure the adequacy in interpersonal relationships will reflect the balance between the generativity and stagnation. The whole mental health aspect and the emotional well-being is connected with this balance. Thus the personality structure itself creates the modality which allows the person to be the source of self-expression or to be a limiting factor of self-directedness. This form of personal relationships is also the ethical modality. This not an added dimension but rather a description of a personality aspect which is essential in the human value development. It expresses the form in which the person is inclined to express him/herself. It gives a form to the manner in which a person exercises responsibility in relation to one's fellow human beings and to God.

Integrated self-determination vs. incarceration in commandments

Human self-realization takes place in its fullness when all the human qualities of the individual are activated and contribute to the perfection of actions and relationships. This fullness is usually not a condition which can be observed in any individual action. It is rather a dynamic expression of the whole personality over a period of time, but which makes itself felt as whole at any given moment. Every moment and every action seem to be firmly anchored in the past, and seem to be confident with regard to the future while remaining flexible and open to change.

Not always does human self-realization reflect this completeness. In many individuals there is a hesitancy or an uncertainty with regard to one's self-expression. The reasons for such hesitancy can vary greatly. It can be an uncertainty about one's own abilities or it can be a feeling of inadequacy vis-a-vis a stronger personality. Sometimes it is a transitory uncertainty, sometimes it seems to be a personal characteristic. Sometimes it can present itself as a need to be totally dependent on outside guidance, while this same guidance is internally, deeply resented. Whether the personality develops according to the favorable conditions or to the unfavorable conditions which are described here, we are always dealing with an approach to life and action which influences the perception of goodness or evil.

This integration or the lack of it is rather a personality trait than simply an acquired habit. It is connected with the structure of the personality. It would seem that the personality structure to which this ethical modality is closest related is the psycho-socio crisis of integrity versus despair or disgust. The quality of integrity as personality structure refers to the completeness of the person. It is not a static condition at which growth has stopped. On the contrary, it is a condition in which growth is consciously and confidently fostered. It is not the absence of struggle and pain, but the past has given confidence in one's ability to cope with problems. The good and the strength of the past together with the courage to act in a cautious wisdom show a wholeness of personality. Such wholeness contributes to a confident approach to life.

The opposite of integrity is the feeling of despair and disgust. This is not a reluctance with regard to certain activities but rather a deeply rooted displeasure with one's own personality. It is, as it were, the feeling of not being integrated. It is the feeling that past, present and future are disconnected and that there is a basic inability to handle normal everyday circumstances. The personality seems to lack the wholeness which provides happiness.

Somewhere between the two extremes of personal integrity or the lack of it lies the degree of efficiency in meeting situations. At this point the individual enters into the inter-human relationships. In the human ability to interact lies also the inclination to perceive certain action as acceptable or inacceptable. The integrated person can be expected to have an ease of self-determination, while the unintegrated person is easily caught in the demands from the outside. These demands are simultaneously wanted and resented. The two extremes or any shade in between do not describe a moral evaluation, but only a modality in which the individual's ethical approach to life is realized.

As I mentioned earlier in this chapter, these ethical modalities are not independent realities which may or may not be present in a human being. Nor are they an exhaustive enumeration of the different forms in which an individual can approach daily life. The ethical modalities try to describe the structural condition with which a person approaches life, or in which the individual can accept him/herself and in which he experiences acceptance by others.

The ethical modalities may show a certain similarity with the stages of moral development which are described in the studies of Lawrence Kohlberg. There is however, a very big difference. Kohlberg studies primarily the degree of moral development in individuals and he classifies them according to the group to which they belong. In this study I look at the structure of the personality and try to understand the basic inclination with which this person is most likely to approach daily life. My search is not for the degree of moral goodness or moral responsibility, but for the characteristics of the personality who tries to act responsibly. The disadvantage of this study is that it is more speculative and escapes measurements, yet it is not less real or less important in interhuman relationships and in the human relationship with God.

In looking back upon these first four chapters, we see a study of the human person as we can perceive this person in his/her daily human interactions. It is, as it were, a picture of the external aspects of the human being, although we deal extensively with the internal and psychological dimensions. I call them external aspects because they show the person whom we can perceive with our senses. But the human being whom we can perceive with our sense is not the complete and total person.

As a Christian I believe in the word of the Bible that God created the human being in His own image, in the image of God. This means that in the *one* and *inseparable* reality of human existence there are two dimensions, namely, the *perceptible* presence in time and space which is simultaneously the visible manifestation of the *invisible* divine reality. The sharing in the divine life which we believe to be real is not a claim of creation but a continuous gift of God. However, because of God's gift this participation in the divine life belongs to human nature. The sharing in the divine life does not flow forth from the structure of the personality, but the divine reality of creative love and self-giving manifests itself in the manner in which the personality is structured.

On the other hand, the fact that we share in God's own life gives to the individual a sense of dignity and value which can have a strong influence upon the growth and development of the personality. In these three aspects of the personality which we have studied so far, the psycho-socio development, the criteria for mental health and the ethical modalities, we have studied the person who relates to God and to fellow human beings. From here we must go to the real purpose of this study, namely, the wholeness which develops when an individual integrates the perceptible dimensions of his/her beings with the sharing of the divine reality. It will be the study of how fundamental Christian virtues are shaped by the human personality and simultaneously contribute to the formation of the personality.

Again I must underline that virtues do not flow forth from the personality structure, but virtuous activity is human and does not take place without or apart from the personality. Virtue and personality are not two forces which either compete or complement each other. They are two aspects of the one human reality, created in the image of God. Perhaps the oneness of the totality escapes us because it belongs to the mystery of being human. To accept a mystery does not mean to deny the reality. The presence of a mystery does not prevent a continuous search for understanding, but it demands that we proceed with reverence and allow ourselves to be guided by faith.

Diagram 3 shows the ethical modalities in a circular presentation to indicate their mutual interdependence and complementarity. The circle surrounds the criteria for mental health and the psychosocio crises to indicate the relationship between the earlier personality dimensions and the ethical modalities. Although each ethical modality seems to be specifically related to specific aspects of criteria for mental health and psycho-socio crises, they do relate to all earlier stages.

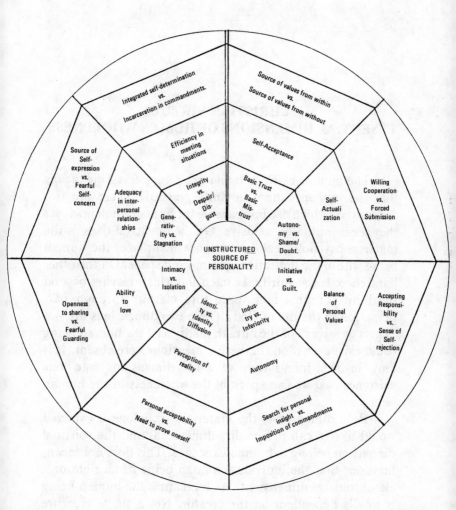

Diagram 3:

Ethical modalities in successive order and in their mutual interdependence
and their relationship with criteria for mental health and stages of
psycho-socio development

5. CHRISTIAN VIRTUES,
ESSENTIAL DIMENSIONS OF HUMAN WHOLENESS

The human being is by nature a mystery. This means that the human cannot be fully grasped. There are two dimensions which are inseparable for human wholeness, yet they seem mutually exclusive. On the one hand there is the material-psychological dimension which places the human being within the limitations of time and space. On the other hand there is the spiritual dimension which reaches beyond the limits of time and space into eternity through participation in the life of God. These two dimensions are not "parts or layers" of the human reality as if the human being could exist even if one of these dimensions were absent. It is only in the integration of both dimensions into one existence that we can speak of the wholeness of the human being.

Both dimensions, the material-psychological (which I would like to call personality-dimension) and the spiritual dimension belong to human existence. This does not mean, however, that the individual human being has a right or a claim to these dimensions. As a creature the human being is totally dependent on the creator. Not a single creature has an ultimate claim on its own existence. Only the creator has the ultimate claim on all that exists. Nonetheless it is often said that the ordinary physical and psychological dimensions fall within the realm (or claim) of the human reality, while the spiritual dimension (participation in the life of God) falls beyond the claim of the human and is purely a gift of God. It is totally beyond the finite condition to share in the life of the infinite.

I believe very strongly that no finite being can claim a right to share in the infinite life. It would seem, however, that we must be careful not to consider the participation in the life of God as a gift which is added to an already existing and complete human reality. God's gift to us is that *we are human.* To be human *includes* the participation in the life of God. This participation in the life of God is simultaneously a reality and a potential. It is a reality in so far that human existence itself is an expression of God's creative self-giving. It is a potential in so far that God's creative self-giving is to be activated within the limits of time and space through the constructive activation of the human potential. Thus any form of human life, even the most incomplete form of the unborn, participates in the life of God. However, whenever the human being develops the capacity to assume personal responsibility (and to the extent of this capacity) the individual must activate his/her human potential. When such a constructive activation of human potential does not take place the individual is personally responsible for the fact that God's life (God's love and goodness) is not concretely expressed at that particular moment of time and space.

It is necessary to carefully keep in mind that the life and love of God do not flow forth from the physical and psychological activities of the human being. On the other hand, it is precisely in the physical and psychological abilities that the divine life and love are manifested in a perceptible human way. This does not mean that the human capacities are merely a tool or a toy in the power of the divine. The activation of the human potential is a totally human responsibility. This human self-activation is also the perceptible concretization of the divine life and love and from this perspective it is totally God's gift. These two dimensions, however, are not two different or separate activities. These two dimensions form one activity for which the human being is responsible, and through which the human being participates in the divine life. We are dealing with the *mystery of being human.*

Truly *human* self-activation then includes all the dimensions of the human reality, namely, the physical, the psychological and the spiritual. Human fullness in its most complete sense includes participation in the life of God. The most complete and the most perfect human being that ever existed was Christ who was fully God and fully human through the mystery of the incarnation. The participation in this mystery of incarnation constitutes the fullness of the human reality. The Second Vatican Council teaches us that "Only in the mystery of the Incarnate Word does the mystery of man take on light."[1]

In daily human conversation there is hardly a word that even comes near to the full expression of this mystery. The word 'human' is normally used to indicate the perceptible and measurable. It is normally used to indicate the limitations of our existence. If we want to indicate the transcendent dimension of our existence we usually use the word 'grace,' which expresses the participation in the life of God. When the human activity is constructive we call this 'virtue.' If such constructive self-activation is expressive of a relationship to God we call it 'supernatural virtue;' otherwise we classify it a 'natural virtue.'

This terminology is accurate and acceptable in so far as it keeps us constantly aware that the created and perceptible human condition is not the same as a participation in the divine life. This participation remains a free gift and a mystery. This same terminology, however, has the disadvantage that it tends to create a dichotomy in our understanding of human wholeness. It tends to present the participation in the divine life as an addition over and above what is human, instead of as the fullness of being human.

Since we want to study the human self-activation in the perspective of the human wholeness it is necessary to study the virtues. The word virtue is meant in this context to comprehend simultaneously the constructive self-realization within human limitations and the manifestation of the participation in the life of God. When we speak about human wholeness these two dimensions cannot be separated.

In an earlier publication I described virtue as "successful human self-fulfillment." [2] In this present discussion I like to use the same description because it expresses the oneness of the two dimensions which must be integrated into the wholeness of human existence as created in the image of God. The description of virtue as "successful human self-fulfillment" has the disadvantage that some people may interpret it as if virtue as a participation in the life of God flows forth from a physical-psychological self-activation. However, this is not what I have in mind. Participation in divine life can never be a result of a physical-psychological self-activation, rather it is through physical-psychological self-activation that the individual brings participation in the divine life into the perceptible human reality.

There is another factor which is important. We must accept that virtue (as human relationship with God) expresses itself as a form of self-activation of the personality of the individual. In addition to this we must also say that the exercise of the virtues influences the shape of the personality or of the human self-activation. It is not only the shape of the personality which influences the form in which the love of God is expressed. The individual's love of God also influences the form and the depth of the individual's total capacity to love. Thus the stronger the personality's ability to love, the deeper his/her love of God can be. The stronger the love of God becomes, the greater will be the openness to love in the personality.

With this mutual influence in mind I want to try to describe some basic traits of human self-activation in relationship to God. First I want to describe the basic virtues which are involved. In the next chapter I will attempt to study how these basic virtues interact with the developmental structures of the human personality.

Human life as a participation in the life of God has two important aspects. First there is the presence of the life of God (through God's gift and through human acceptance), and secondly the activation of this life in human self-expression. These two aspects are not independent of each other. Whenever a person is able to assume personal responsibility for his/her activities, he/she must be willing (or at least not wilfully oppose) to express the presence of God in their own life, otherwise their life is in fact not manifesting God's love in human reality. On the other hand, the human activity cannot be expressive of God's life unless this life is there through God's gift to the individual.

The presence of God's life in the human being is usually expressed through the concept of grace. The basic human reply, as a direct expression of God's presence and of personal participation in God's life, is called the activity of the divine virtues. The human response to God which expresses itself in interhuman relationship and in the use of the material world, is usually called the activity of the moral virtues. These virtues are descriptive of the constructive value of human self-activation and of the degree in which a person expresses through his/her human goodness, the love and goodness of God.

Christian virtues are not independent entities which are or can be juxtapositioned. Neither is it possible to develop one virtue independently of the others, yet, they are not the same and each virtue can be described individually. In the following pages I will try to describe eight virtues. This is not meant to be a theological treatise, nor is it meant to be a complete description or an exhaustive enumeration of the Christian virtues. Rather it is meant to be a vision of the basic characteristics of a human being in his/her personal relationship with God.

FAITH

Faith is often understood as an intellectual exercise. It is then equated with "to believe something or someone." The word "to believe" can vary in its meaning from "having an opinion (but being quite uncertain) about something" to "being deeply convinced." Faith has an element of knowledge which is presented from an outside source and which, at least at this moment, cannot be fully grasped by the individual. These two elements, coming from an outside source and escaping full human understanding, are important in understanding faith as a dimension in the human relationship with God. Faith does not originate in the human, and when it can be fully comprehended by the human intellect it stops being faith.

Faith is not merely an intellectual exercise, nor even the intellectual act of accepting the information which the other (God, Church authorities) present to us. There is a deeper dimension, as Karl Rahner says; "Faith is never awakened by someone having something communicated to him purely from the outside, addressed solely to the naked understanding as such. To lead to faith (or rather to its further explicit stage), is always to assist understanding of what has already been experienced in the depth of human reality as grace (i.e., as in absolutely direct relation to God)."[3]

Faith has, therefore, these totally intertwined aspects. It has information from the outside and an inner experience. This inner experience is brought to awareness through information from the outside source. Again quoting Rahner we can say that: "the primary approach to faith is man's direct confrontation with himself in his whole human nature as free and responsible and thereby with the incomprehensible ground of his human reality, called God."[4] Faith is the involvement of the whole person. It is the human confrontation with him/herself recognizing one's total dependence on the creator. It also means to recognize and accept that there is a dimension which is real and which belongs to human wholeness, yet which depth escapes human comprehension.

In this perspective faith becomes a life-expression which includes a commitment. This means that through faith there is a need for self-realization of human wholeness in which the perceptible human dimensions are integrated with the dimensions which escape human comprehension. The expression of faith becomes the meeting place of the self-manifestation of God to the human and of the self-giving of the human to God.

Faith is a gift of God (a self-giving of God) to the person so that the individual can begin to live consciously a personal relationship to God. In both aspects, as a gift and as a task, faith is perceived and expressed according to the personality structures of the individual. Faith, while surpassing any human claim, remains a deeply human reality.

HOPE

"It might seem unnecessary to go on and speak of hope after faith, since faith, if lived out to the fullest, includes hope."[5] This brief quote from the New Catechism highlights a very important perspective of the virtue of hope. Hope is more than the well-founded expectation that God will be faithful to his promises and grant us eternal life if we live according to his commandments.

The basic elements of hope are very similar to the basic elements of faith. In the virtue of hope we accept a total dependence on God and as well as our human limitations. Hope contains a vision of the future in which the integration of the human with the divine must be realized. Hope accepts this integration as God's gift to the human, and also that this integration is dependent on human self-activation according to one's capacities. Hope bases itself upon the belief that the human shares in the life of God, but that the presence of God's life is made dependent on the human will to integrate as well as on the self-giving of God. Hope is the conscious possession of what is to be integrated into the future.

When the experience of human limitation inclines the individual to overlook or to deny the presence of God with us, it is hope that can look to the future and to the wholeness of human existence. We may say that: "Through hope, faith avoids the mistake of taking the hiddenness of God for absence."[6] The virtue of hope is included in the virtue of faith. Hope is that element of faith which asks for the activation of the human potential to express participation in the life of God. Hope is in a very special way the virtue of the human being as "pilgrim on earth."

Obviously, hope cannot exist without faith. The two virtues are often presented in the scriptures as being so closely interrelated that they seem to coincide.[7] Yet for everyday human life, hope seems to draw out of the human reality the specific activation through which the individual responds to the God whose presence he accepts in faith. Hope is also the source of an underlying security that despite one's human limitations one has value before God. While accepting the absence of the integration of the material-psychological aspects of human existence with the spiritual dimensions of our being, hope contains the certainty that this integration will be achieved through the faithful activation of one's potential. Hope does not confuse the divine with the created, but integrates these two dimensions by the activation-in-faith of the human potential.

LOVE

Faith and hope are two inseparable moments of the one act, of which (initial) love is the integrating center. The juxtaposition of the three theological virtues caused a certain amount of obscurity with regard to the intrinsic unity of these three virtues. The unity of the three theological virtues is very important and may not be overlooked. In these three virtues we have the acceptance of God's presence with us, the activation of our human potential, and the reaching out of the whole human existence to God. Love in its deepest meaning is an act of self-giving.

Love in its completeness is a giving and a response. It is an interaction in which each of the participants is both giver and receiver. Love as a theological virtue speaks about the human relationship with God in which the poles of mutual self-giving—God and the creature—are on totally different levels. It is necessary to look at each of the poles separately.

Many definitions of love are possible, but all seem to have a common element. Love is the personal reaching out of the giver for the enrichment of the receiver, and in this process of reaching out the giver also is enriched. This basic element can be applied to the love of God for humanity and of the human beings for God.

God's love for humanity is a personal reaching out on his part for the enrichment of the receiver. On the part of God the enriching reaching out means a communication of being (or a calling into existence) with regard to humanity. It is more than simply communication of existence; things and animals also exist through God's gift. For the human being this communication of divine self-giving means a participation in divine life itself. Greater love cannot be imagined, since nothing can exceed a communication of existence and participation in the divine life. It is the highest possible enrichment of the human being, and (speaking in human language) it is an enrichment of God through activation of his power of love and creation.

On the part of the human being there is a similar need to reach out. This reaching out to God gives an actual shape to the self-giving of God to the human. The same activation also creates the fullness of the human being. Thus love itself is the perfection of existence since it is an activation which creates a fullness of giver and receiver both.

In the perspective of human life, love is the perfection of interhuman relationships. Love contains many aspects. It sees realistically one's own incompleteness and one's need to reach out creatively and constructively. It perceives one's own value which can enrich other persons in specific ways. It comprehends in others the need to receive according to the other's value and personality. Love has a deep respect for the self and the other simultaneously. Thus in interhuman relationships genuine love has two dimensions which may not be separated. There is the acquisition of a good for the fulfillment of "self," and at the same time a contribution to the completeness of the other. Genuine love is always "unselfish" in so far as it is directed to another and to the other's well being. On the other hand, genuine love is never self-diminutive. It accepts personal growth and satisfaction as an essential dimension of love. It is the divine commandment to love God with one's whole mind and heart and with all one's strength. This is how total dependence on God is manifested; it is also the only manner in which the human being can become fully human.

In love, therefore, we see the integration of the acceptance of God's presence-in-faith and the human self-activation-in-hope in a direct reaching out to the creator. Thus in the unity of the three theological virtues we can see the participation in the life of God. It is a participation which remains totally God's gift but which demands a total human commitment. It becomes the integration of the finite with the infinite. However, the expression of this integration happens in the finite dimensions of human existence which receive a specific strength and form of development through participation in the divine life. This fundamentally integrated human being reaches out to and interacts with the surrounding world and with other human beings.

HONESTY & JUSTICE

Faith, hope and love are to be understood as a unity which constitute the human being in the participative condition of sharing in the life of God. It is accurate to say that they constitute the human being on the supernatural level. Yet, we must also say that this participation in the life of God constitutes the fullness of being human. Thus these virtues belong to the human being. Without minimizing the reality of God's gift to the human, we also must dare to accept them as natural to human existence. Through the virtues of faith, hope and love a person has the foundation for making the whole human self-expression a manifestation of God's presence and love in human reality.

In this perspective one of the first requirements is the recognition of one's own condition. This means the recognition of one's personal value in relation to one's self and to others. The recognition of one's personal value demands an honesty which is an attitude of accepting reality as it is. It demands the acceptance of one's own goodness as simultaneously God's gift and one's own responsibility. It demands also the acceptance of one's limitations as the reality in which God's goodness can be expressed. These limitations are the boundaries for the capacities which translate God's goodness into the language of human behavior and which give shape to this translation. They are the created expression of our being and simultaneously they are the product of our responses to God's invitation to us. To recognize this condition and to accept it as a basis for further activity and self-expression is an expression of honesty. It is an expression of truth toward oneself.

Honesty as a truthful acceptance of one's total dependence on God and of one's personal value does not stop with one's own personality. It reaches beyond oneself into the community. Honesty appreciates the value and ability of others. It accepts others for their own value and is willing to contribute to the growth and development of those with whom one lives. Honesty expects to be accepted and respected by others on one's own value. Thus it becomes inseparably interlocked with justice.

Justice is usually understood as knowingly and

willingly attributing to others what is theirs and contributing to their growth and development. The most basic element of justice is truth. Justice is the recognition of the abilities and needs of others. Simultaneously it is the recognition of one's own abilities to respond to these needs or to activate the abilities of others. Justice is the recognition that one does not stand alone in this world, but that one is called to express in conjunction with others the greatness of the creator. A sense of justice is a source of responsibility toward oneself and others.

It could be a cause for wonder that the virtues of honesty and justice are presented as a unit. The reason is that both virtues center around the basic element of truth. Both express themselves in three mutually integrative aspects. They focus on the recognition of concrete situations, conditions or values in individuals and in society. They require a willingness to respond to such concrete situations, conditions and values in a constructive activity. Finally, they lead persons to experience this recognition and response as a participation in the creative and redemptive self-expression of God through Christ. In a very real sense honesty and justice are the basis for active involvement in virtuous (wholesome or holy) human self-expression.

TEMPERANCE

Temperance is easily understood in a negative sense as a curtailing of one's desires or satisfactions. In this perspective it suggests a restriction of pleasure seeking. This understanding has a high degree of accuracy but leads easily to misrepresentations. It would perhaps be better to describe temperance as: a search for balance in the total realization of all the dimensions of human values. In other places I have indicated that in human existence there are three major categories of value-dimensions. These are the physical, psychological and spiritual value dimensions. The physical dimensions refer to the human presence in time and space. The psychological dimensions deal with the interhuman relationships, while the spiritual dimensions are concerned with the human self-expression in relationship to God.

Between these value dimensions there is a balance which is needed for the growth and development of these values. An overstressing of material well-being can easily lead to personal satisfaction with disregard for the well-being of others, or it can lead to a misuse of others for one's own benefit. An overstressing of certain psychological values (such as self-image, acceptability with others, and so forth) can easily make a person very self-conscious. These concerns tend to turn a person into him/herself. Personal needs are then often satisfied at the cost of others.

Spiritual values can never be overstressed, but they can be misunderstood. A person can never be too spiritual, but it is possible to develop a so-called spirituality which denies the role and value of the physical and psychological dimensions of human existence. This denial could easily mean a disruption of the human reality and prevent a total response to God's gift to the human being.

As human beings we all experience our existence in time and space. We all search for complementation through interaction with other persons. These physical and psychological dimensions are within the immediate realm of human awareness. Within these dimensions the individual experiences well and woe, sadness and joy, pleasure and pain. The human has, therefore, the inclination to satisfy these needs whenever they are felt.

The inclination toward physical/psychological satisfaction contains a constant pressure toward a one-sided development. The spiritual meaning of human existence does not flow forth from physical or psychological dimensions. The spiritual meaning is experienced *within* these dimensions, but it is a specific human quality which will remain underdeveloped when material or measurable aspects dominate human life. Thus external perfection can hide a defective totality.

Temperance is a search for balance between the various value dimensions in human existence. Temperance is not restrictive. When temperance is experienced as restrictive, it is because one approaches it from the viewpoint of unbalanced demands for perceptible satisfactions. In the true meaning of human development temperance is the immediate consequence and activation of honesty and justice. Temperance is the insight into the truth of the human reality in its wholeness. It is the concerted effort to allow every dimension to develop according to its own function in the human existence. Temperance, when correctly understood, contributes to the full and mutually constructive integration of the perceptible with the spiritual dimensions of human life.

GENEROSITY

The search for balance in the activation of human value dimensions will remain incomplete without a true generosity. Generosity is usually understood as the readiness to give of one's own goods to others who are in need. Thus it seems to have its emphasis on the external aspects of human self-expression. In reality this is not completely accurate. Generosity presupposes several underlying attitudes which touch very closely the spiritual dimensions of the human being.

Generosity is based upon the proper attitude toward

material goods. It includes the recognition of the relativity of their value and it includes the acceptance of their social meaning. Thus generosity presupposes a grateful acceptance of one's own personal value and one's own meaningfulness for others. It is a readiness to share of oneself with others constructively so that others can benefit by this sharing. Generosity does not calculate the amount one can gain personally. Instead, it is concerned about the growth which can take place in others. Generosity is exactly the opposite of the tendency to use other persons for one's own purposes. Generosity is built on respect for oneself and for others, and it displays a trust in the basic goodness of all.

Every form of self-giving is based upon honesty and justice, because it must recognize the value of persons and the ways in which human interaction contributes to growth. Self-giving is a life giving process. The more an individual is in possession of his/her own personality, that is, the more a person is convinced of his/her deep personal value, the greater will the ability be to contribute constructively to the growth of the other. Some people seem very generous, but their generosity lacks sensitivity for the needs of the others. Their sole concern is that they themselves may feel good. The well-being of the others is only a secondary aspect. Such generosity seems to be a search for control over others rather than a contribution to their growth.

The virtue of generosity, therefore, does not simply mean a readiness to give of one's material possessions to alleviate the needs of others. Generosity is a creative self-giving in which the deepest layers of one's own personal life are enriched because they are activated in the constructive relationship with other persons. Generosity demands the ability to share one's deepest self with others.

FORTITUDE

The search for balance in human value-dimensions and growth-directed reaching out to others demands a continuity. Human life is not simply a matter of maintaining existence. Human life means growth, and growth implies a constant change. Change carries along with it the uncertainty of the next step, a tearing away from the familiar and the risk of entering into the unknown. This whole process demands a specific kind of strength in the individual.

The strength that is needed is more than stubborness and perseverance. It is an attitude which grasp one's personal development in the past and estimates its importance and strength. It is viewing one's own qualities and abilities and their developmental potential. It is necessary to be honest when reflecting on one's own abilities and limitations in order to activate them in a continuous effort of self-realization.

The virtue of fortitude is present and active throughout all the dimensions of human and Christian growth. It has a special importance when a person is faced with difficulties. This strength in difficulties is important in every dimension of human growth, but particularly in the development of Christian courage. In a world which by its nature tends to cling to the external and to seek satisfaction in material and psychological fulfillment, Christian fidelity demands special strength. Christian fidelity demands a deep awareness of the spiritual dimension and value in human existence. It demands special courage to continuously recognize the value of the spiritual reality and make this the fulfillment of human wholeness without rejecting the value of the material aspects.

Fortitude enables a person to give continuous witness to the truth of human wholeness which is revealed in Christ.

It is the quality which ultimately arranges the life of the individual so that Christ's life is manifested, even, if necessary, at the cost of one's own life. Fortitude is not only necessary in the exceptional instances of martyrdom. The virtue of fortitude is an indispensable human and Christian quality which allows the continuous expression of the human totality. It is the courage to endure pain so that good and fulfillment may follow.

PRUDENCE

Christian virtues, just as human qualities, are mutually interdependent. The development of one includes the development of others. Yet, in this mutual interdependence there is a certain binding force or an ability to bring these qualities or virtues together; to oversee their activity; to sense the direction into which their activation might lead; and to react constructively for the benefit of oneself and of others.

Prudence exercises a certain degree of caution, but it does not prevent one from acting spontaneously or from taking risks. Prudence prevents one from being carried away by sudden emotions and impulses which would lead to harmful self-expression. However, formed by past experiences, prudence is able to project the likelihood of success in special forms of self-activation. There is also a certain ability to evaluate possible consequences when an activity would be unsuccessful. In the balancing of these two possibilities, prudence is able to take risks intelligently. Prudence is a virtue of maturity. It grasps the meaning and direction of life and accordingly, leads to the full realization of the human potential.

Though a virtue of maturity, prudence is not merely a gift for a certain age level. It is rather the result of a continuous alertness to the meaning and the demands of life at every age. In the perspective of the developmental stages of Christian virtues prudence emerges as a dimension of the perfection of all virtues. Undoubtedly, the perfection of every virtue is love, but in the virtuous activity itself it is prudence that leads all virtues into the harmony of full human action.

The acceptance of self in honesty and justice, the form of balance between human value-dimensions, the degree of self-giving and the depth of self-communication, the strength for continued self realization, all these are aspects which ask for a vision of the human/Christian totality, of the meaning of human life, and of the ultimate vocation of human existence. It is this wholeness which is grasped by the virtue of prudence and which develops slowly through faithful responses to the opportunities of constructive self-expression.

The above description of eight Christian virtues is not intended as a theological study of the virtues. Nor is it meant to be an exhaustive enumeration of Christian virtues. It is only intended as a description of how a human being might act when activating the potential of his/her own personality in a search for human wholeness. The descriptive presentation of Christian virtues, however, is meant to observe such a person from the perspective of his/her God-orientation. It is meant to see this person in the acceptance of personal value and dependence (faith), while looking forward to fulfillment despite limitations (hope) in self-giving to the creator (love).

In the expression of daily life such a person accepts the reality of individual and interpersonal values and relations (honesty & justice). There is a personal reaching out to others (generosity), despite occuring and often frightening difficulties (fortitude). Thus the human wholeness—man-

God-relationship—is seen as the goal and objective of Christian activity (prudence).

In the earlier part of this work (chapters one thru four) I have tried to present the human personality which we meet in the concrete circumstances of every day life. The study of the developmental stages were only descriptive of the many possibilities and influences which ultimately constitute a human being. But this same human being with this particular form and structure of personality responds also to God, either by accepting God's reality and God's love or by rejecting it totally or to a degree. Whether it be an acceptance or rejection, it is always an expression of the personality. Thus the virtues and their external manifestation are inseparably interlocked with personality development. Simultaneously, however, the developmental stages (and the final form) of the personality is also inseparably intertwined with the growth and development of the Christian virtues. There is, as it were, a continuous tension between the finite and infinite in their development and interlocking. In this tension the human being is created and becomes actively the image of God (or refuses to be this image). This creative tension is the subject of the next chapter.

6. CREATIVE TENSION BETWEEN
THE DEVELOPMENT OF PERSONALITY
STRUCTURES AND CHRISTIAN VIRTUES

The previous chapter opened with the statement that the human being is by nature a mystery because it unites inseparably the finite and the infinite. We may never lose sight of this dimension. To consider the virtues as merely favorable psychological developments would mean to eliminate from the human being participation in the life of God. To consider Christian virtues and participation in the divine life as additions to an already complete human existence would make participation in the divine life something which is by its nature alien to human nature. The human qualities would then become merely means through which divine life operates in this world. Human participation in the divine life would then be no greater than the role of a brush in the hands of a painter.

Human participation in the life of God, however, is much more than the relationship between artist and instrument. The Book of Genesis tells us that God created the human being in his own image, in the image of God (Gn. 1:27). St. John tries to tell us in many different ways that, if we believe, we live in God and God in us (cf. the letters of St. John). The scriptures credit a much higher dignity to the human being than merely being an instrument. It is a true participation in which the human assumes responsibility for his/her personal life, not only for physical existence but also for spiritual well-being.

Participation in the life of God remains God's gift to the human in every aspect and at every moment. This gift is so total and so complete that it even includes the responsibility as to whether or not an individual will manifest at a given moment God's life in human dimensions. Just as God is continuously the source of his own being and existence, so also must every individual be personally responsible for his/her self-expression. Obviously, human responsibility can be exercised only within the limitations of human existence. Human development and growth is self-realization in time and space. Development and growth may be called creation in slow motion. The human is the mystery in which the divine manifests itself. Therefore, the human is the mystery which is most itself when it manifests a greatness beyond the perceptible. The human is the mystery which is most itself when it presents the infinite in the finite dimensions of time and space.

However much the virtues may be God's gift, they grow and develop in and through human activity. It is a form of growth and development in which the human and the divine form one principle of operation. The developmental stages of the personality are the way in which an individual can, at a certain moment, perceive him/herself and relate to others. These same stages of personality development are also the form in which this individual expresses, manifests or lives his/her participation in the life of God. Simultaneously, the participation in the life of God gives direction and depth to the developmental stages of this person. This means that there is a continuous interaction between the development of the personality and of the virtues.

It can hardly be repeated often enough and explicitly

enough that the spiritual dimension of human existence—the participation in the life of God—does not originate as a developmental process of human growth. This participation simply has no human origin. It is a gift of God to the human which grows and develops inseparably from human effort and human self-determination. However, this process of spiritual growth and development is so totally interwoven with the development of the personality characteristics that many people are inclined to put them on the same level. To do this would be a very serious mistake.

Karl Rahner warns us that "Because man today is slowly acquiring the possibility of understanding and controlling himself like a grandiose computer, he is horribly tempted to understand himself *only* as a computer."[1] There is in the human being an area which is very real but which can never be described in the terms of the external, calculable elements which fall within the limits of computer programming. Rahner continues saying: "Prayer is precisely the one realization of the one, single subject as such, which can never be the object of exact sciences."[2] What can be said about prayer must also be said about the development of virtues in human life. The nature, the degree and strength of participation in God's life through the life of virtues escapes completely any form of human calculation. The expression and development of the virtues, however, can only be understood in their relation to the development of the human personality. This relationship we want to study in the following pages.

FAITH IN HUMAN PERSPECTIVE

I start from the assumption that faith is a gift of God to the human. It is presented to the individual in the human condition of his/her being and, consequently, it is received in the same individual human condition. Faith has, therefore, a double perspective. It is God's self-manifestation to the individual and the individual's recognition of his/her own dependence of God. Both dimensions take place in the human reality. Faith is expressed according to the personality structure of the individual and the personality structure finds a goal and directive for self-realization in the presence of faith.

Although faith is not merely an act of the intellect, it cannot exist without some form of intellectual knowledge. This requirement of knowledge may make us think that the awakening of faith is directly related to the awakening of the intelligence. By the same principle one might be inclined to think that the growth and development of faith will take place according to the developmental process of the intellect. This would mean that the greater the knowledge, particularly the knowledge of doctrine, the deeper faith would be. In daily human life there seems to be an inclination to assume that faith deepens when knowledge increases.

However indispensable knowledge may be for faith, it is only one aspect of faith. Perhaps we may even say that it is not even the most important aspect. Faith is not so much a knowledge of God but rather a personal acceptance of human dependence on God. I call it a "personal acceptance of dependence" because it includes an intellectual and affective attitude in which the individual leans toward a personal dedication to God. This affective element does not necessarily mean an emotional affectivity. It is rather the leaning of a person toward specific dedication and direction of life. It is a response to the attraction and meaningfulness of the good of one's existence. In other words, it is directly related to the self-acceptance of one's personality.

The personal acceptance of dependence is a structural

form of the human personality. It means a certain balance in which an individual evaluates his/her personal value and importance and simultaneously reflects this personal value in the perspective of other people. It means recognizing that one has value and that this value finds its proper realization in relation with others. The strength and the depth of faith is closely related to the degree of the individual's personal dedication for this form of self-realization. The depth of faith depends on the degree to which an individual is capable of accepting his/her dependence on God.

Dependence on God can express itself in many different forms. It can be a feeling of trust, encouragement and personal value. It can also be an attitude of fear, distrust and rejection. Whatever the attitude may be will also be the expression of one's faith. Some persons look at God as a concerned and loving father. Others understand him as a harsh judge whose punitive mentality is always alert for possible faults or sins.

Such very different expressions of faith in the same God is not because God's gift to each individual was different. It would be more accurate to say that God gives himself personally and totally to each individual but each one receives and responds according to his/her own personality. The trusting person can be aware of a total dependence on God and find in this dependence a sense of happiness and dignity. The distrusting person is more likely to experience this total dependence as a source of fear and anxiety.

If we want to understand faith in human perspective then we must first of all see and understand the structure of the individual personality. The basic attitude of the individual in his/her relationship with other persons will very strongly influence the form in which this individual's faith in God is expressed. Although the attitude of an individual is a continuously growing and unfolding reality of life, it does reflect the earlier stages of human development. The first of the psycho-socio crisis—basic trust vs. basic mistrust—remains an important factor in the development of the personality. Consequently, this tension between trust and mistrust also remains a very important factor in the manner in which the gift of faith is received as well as in the manner in which the individual responds to it.

Faith plays an important role at every stage of life and development, but the basic form in which this intellectual and effective attitude is realized is best understood if we grasp the importance and role of the earliest stages of human development. The psycho-socio crises of basic trust vs. basic mistrust which indicates the tension and the balance of one's ability to rely on others or to guard against them is not only a determinant for relationships between human beings. The basic trust vs. mistrust also has its importance in the relationship with God. God is understood and approached as a person who is outside oneself. However deeply a person may be convinced of God's presence within him/her, Faith never allows a personal identification with God. God remains the other. In the relationship with God the same balance between relying on God and guarding against him will be expressed.

Immediately connected with this balance and tension is the degree of self-acceptance. For the self-accepting person, reliance on others is no threat but rather a form of self-fulfillment. This sense of self-worth, which is intimately connected with the degree of one's self-acceptance, also manifests itself in the relationship with God. Where there is a deep sense of personal value the dependence on others becomes a reaching out to others for personal fulfillment. It is not an expression of weakness that seeks completion by possessing the other, nor is it a sub-missiveness which means a loss of identity. It is rather a reaching out in which both giver and receiver are enriched.

When the source of values lies within the person then the reaching out to the other as an expression of depen-dence means an activation of inner goodness rather than a plea to fill an emptiness. This is what describes the ex-pression of faith in God. It is the degree of personal trust and self-acceptance with an inner value that reaches out to God as a self-activation in which God's presence is manifested. Or it can be the lack of trust, self-acceptance and inner value which reaches out in fear and deepens the anxiety in so doing.

From another vantage point, however, we can see how faith can be a source of strength and of positive re-inforcement of personal value. Faith is not only an affective attitude which determines the nature and form of human dependence on God. Faith is also an insight. Accurate and clear insights are one of the basic means for changing attitudes and inclinations. The better we know a person-in-authority, the more we may feel at ease in his/her presence, or vice versa. So also, the more one can see through faith the nature and the goodness of God, the more one might feel at ease with being totally dependent. Faith can convey the insight that our total dependence on God is also the source of the highest human dignity. This sense of dignity contributes directly to a personal sense of trust, self-acceptance and inner value. Thus at the basis of the per-sonalith there is a direct relationship between the per-sonality structure and faith. Faith and personality become two aspects of the same human reality in which the in-dividual person relates to others and to God.

Obviously, faith does not work only in the primitive stages of the personality. Faith works all throughout life.

Every stage and every degree of development can be influenced by faith just as every stage is influenced by the earliest developmental stages. This influence remains to a large degree under the control of the individual. Faith is never imposed. Even when a doctrine can be forced upon an individual, the inner attitude and adherence remain a personal decision. However, if we believe that the human being is created in the image of God then the refusal to accept a total dependence on God would mean a choice to remain incomplete and unfulfilled.

Faith does not stand in the way of human development. Faith does not impose laws or limitations. On the contrary, it activates within the human infinite dimensions and tendencies. Faith inspires personal development and initiative; it gives a sense of identity, leads to intimate friendships and integrates persons and society. At the same time it warns against self-centeredness, isolation and misuse of others. Faith is the basis on which a personality, who can accept the human in its fullness without being threatened by the greatness of the creator, is built.

HOPE, THE VIRTUE OF HUMAN LIMITATIONS

In a somewhat irreverent manner we may say that hope does not stand on its own feet. Hope presupposes faith and leads to love. In a certain way it is an in-between virtue. Hope is there because the individual accepts in faith the presence of God and the total dependence of the human being on God. Simultaneously, hope experiences human limitations and grasps the human insufficiency regarding the task of expressing God's life in human dimensions. Hope has as its human foundation the existential and experiential vision which states that it is beyond creature's potential to live out the divine image which the human being is called to be.

This vision of the human limitations helps us understand that hope is a divine virtue. It grasps simultaneously the extent of the human limitations and the call to divine self-expression. Thus it is an activation of limited potential to wander into the unknown. It is the activation of a finite potential to express the infinite.

An in-depth vision of faith is a frightening experience. Faith sees simultaneously the human little-ness and the divine infinitude. Faith grasps more or less the extremes of this reality and the human inability to cope with it. The presence of the divine, simultaneously hidden and manifested in created limitations, may easily be perceived as mere hiddenness. In this perception, faith would lead to despair. It is here that hope enters into the created realm as an aspect of activated faith. Hope prevents that the hiddenness of God be taken for absence. It also prevents created, limited existence to be rejected as unworthy. Hope accepts the human, however incomplete it may be, and works with it confidently to reach the unreachable. Because of hope, the individual human being, as it were, possesses what is the object of his/her striving, namely, a participation in the divine life through the faithful activation of human potential. Hope accepts the gift of God's presence and integrates it into human self-expression.

Hope, therefore, plays an indispensable role as long as a person is subject to physical, created limitations. This means that hope is an essential dimension of the human relationship with God for every person on earth. Hope is not the basis of the human relationship with God, but as soon as the basis of faith is there, hope must permeate every subsequent dimension of the human response to God. Hope belongs to every phase of life. It guides the activity, it trusts one's personal identity and looks with expectation to the intended (hoped for) results of personal dedication.

In and through this total personal involvement, hope remains God's gift to the individual enabling him/her to express a life-orientation which reaches into the divine as into its ultimate fulfillment. Hope is then, a self-communication of the divine creative power which can accept the slow movement of growth as creation in slow motion, which leads to the final unification of the finite with the infinite. Hope is the virtue of self-activation for spiritual self-expression. Its expression in the various dimensions of the personality may therefore be best understood in terms of basic human self-actualization.

Human self-actualization in its most original form goes back to the psycho-socio stage of autonomy vs. shame. At this stage the individual person ventured into the unknown, guided by his/her own initiative. It was simultaneously an exercise in motor functioning and a reaching into the realm beyond its own perception. The degree of experience of acceptance by others became a confirmation of the degree of personal acceptability or of a sense of personal rejectibility. This early stage determined whether or not self-actualization could be allowed and whether it would be possible to willingly cooperate with others or whether perhaps rebellion should be preferrable and cooperation accepted only as a forced submission.

This basic relational attitude of self-worth and cooperation—or self-rejection and fear to be dependent—is also the human reality in which self-realization-in-faith must take place. Some persons can see no other God than the one who wants to humiliate and punish them. They may subject in fear as long as they experience material security. They may sink into despair when God is left as their only hope. Other persons, on the contrary, gratefully accept their abilities, however limited they may be, and they can gratefully accept the dependence on others which is supporting rather than limiting. They consider cooperation an expression of respect and an increase of personal dignity rather than a rejection of personal value.

Hope does not result from this psychological stage but in its expression in daily life and in its impact upon human/religious activities, it seems to follow the pattern of this personal balance. This same form offers the opportunity for growth. The experience of goodness and the deepening of faith can lead to a greater trust in God. This trust in God is an acceptance of dependence as well as an acceptance of personal value and leads to a deeper security in interpersonal relationships. Participation in the life of God has a direct influence on the positive development of the personality. When the structure of the personality is the form in which hope is received and expressed, the virtue of hope becomes a major force in the development of the personality.

LOVE, UNIFICATION AND FULFILLMENT

The human being is by nature relational. This can hardly be surprising when we accept that the very origin of the human is a relational reality. In the beginning of this book I tried to describe creation as a self-manifestation of God. Creation is a self-communication in which the creator communicates existence to a being that never was before and that now uniquely expresses the creator's life. Thus the act of creation itself is a relational act. The human being exists only in relationships because creation is not one act in time and space but a continuous activity. The human being exists because of an ongoing relationship with God. Therefore, created in the image of God can not be real unless the human self-expression also manifests an ongoing, constructive relationship.

Human relationship with the creator is a dependent

relationship. This means that the human being is totally and continuously dependent on God. It is not a sort of dependency in which the two principals, the giver and the receiver (the creator and the creature) can stand aloof from each other. It is a communication of existence. This means that the creator is by necessity most intimately united with the creature because the creator is the life of the creature. On the other hand, the creature is also most intimately united with the creator because the creature lives by the same life.

Creation is an independent act of personal responsibility. In the deepest sense of the word, creation is life communicating life. According to human dimensions, creation is the highest form of reaching out to others. This is the image in which the human has been created. Therefore, the human being is called by its very essence to express this form of self-actualization. The more a person actualizes his/her own potential as a human being in the fullest sense of the word, the more clearly and completely will the image of God (or rather the life of God) be lived and manifested.

From this very summary description it becomes clear that every person has by necessity an intimate relationship with God. Whether a person wants to acknowledge and accept this relationship or not does not change the fact of its existence. However, it seems obvious that a grateful acceptance and acknowledgement of this relationship creates a relationship which is more deeply human and expresses a greater human completeness. Such an acknowledgement activates and directs the human intelligence toward the full truth of human existence. Such an acknowledgement is the total dedication of the person to the fullness of his/her own being. Such acknowledgement and dedication is an expression of true love.

True love acknowledges one's own value as well as one's limitations. Love acknowledges the need for others not as objects to be possessed or used, but as equals who complement and enrich. Love also acknowledges the value of others and their limitations. Love recognizes how both partners receive in giving and give in receiving because in love they give and receive themselves and each other. In their unification they reach completion and fulfillment. In the total self-communication the creator becomes himself as creator while the human being in the full recognition of his/her own reality becomes fully human.

Obviously, this ability in the creature to love (to extend itself totally to) the creator and to be unified with the creator is in itself a gift which the creature cannot claim. It is a gratuitous gift and an expression of the deepest love on the part of God for humanity. It demands the same full response on the part of individual human beings. In human beings, however, this response in love is not possible unless there is a recognition of the total human dependence on God in faith. Love is then the perfection of faith since love builds upon the acceptance of dependence and finds personal fullness in being oneself in total dependence.

In the human condition on earth love needs the active presence and involvement of hope. Love is not a dream but the reality of human limitations directing themselves in total surrender to the creator. Love includes an awareness of personal value within the human limitations and can currender oneself in unreserved trust. In the human condition, love is the perfection of hope.

However idealistic we may try to describe the meaning and reality of love, it must express itself in the human interchange in which one person relates to another in personal self-extension. For some persons it seems to be an easy, almost natural gesture to extend oneself to others without imposing or to accept others without possessiveness. Other persons seem to experience a certain hesitancy as if they are not sure how trustworthy the other person is. Finally, there are individuals who seem to be closed to others. When they extend themselves they want to dominate, when they receive from others they want to possess. Yet in each of these three (clear-cut) possible expressions of interhuman relationships, each individual is convinced that he/she expresses genuine love. Love is expressed according to the structure of the personality.

A reflection on the structure of each of these three forms of self-expression seems to indicate that all have a basic concurrence of two fundamental components. In each of them there is a special form of self-acceptance (self-value) which ranges from a deep sense of personal value to a feeling of deep personal unworthiness. Simultaneously, there seems to be in each of them a particular way of confidence in one's self-expression. The first seems to have no fear of either approaching others or being approached. This ease of self-expression seems to be less in the subsequent instances. Love then, is the form of self-giving which balances the degree of personal self-acceptance and self-confidence in acting into one personal expression.

Love is a dimension which relates to all aspects of human existence and it encompasses every human potential. Its basic structure, however, seems to be derived from the combination of the individual's personal value and self-confidence. This means that love finds its basic form in the stage of psycho-socio development which is constituted by the tension in which personal initiative and guilt search for a balance. It is the tension which both urges one to reach out and is at the same time the basic feeling of personal rejectibility when one does reach out to others. It is the basic attitude of reaching and offering oneself to others as a gift of value or the attitude of submitting others to oneself in order to gain personal value.

Expressions of love for God follow the pattern of interhuman expressions of love. St. John suggested: If you want to know how much you love God, see how much you love your neighbor. This does not simply refer to the degree or amount of love; it also speaks about the manner in which we love. Our love for God is God's gift to us, it is also our self-expression in relation to God. When as human beings, we are capable of deeper love then we are also capable of deeper love for God. Conversely, if our love of God deepens through the experience of goodness or other religious experiences, then our human capacity for loving will also increase and deepen.

Such increase of love strengthens faith and hope and gives a sense of greater personal value. Greater acceptability deepens self-confidence, leads to activity and recognizes one's own identity. It allows a sense of intimacy and brings all human qualities together into one integrated personality. Love is the experience of the oneness of the divine and the human, and thus communicates to individuals and society a sense of fulfillment and wholeness.

Faith, Hope and Love are normally understood as the three divine or theological virtues because their "object" is God. They are also a direct communication of the life of God. I think that the foregoing pages help us see what these statements mean. Faith is the recognition of God as the source of human existence. Hope is the human effort to reach out to God despite human limitations and inability. Love is the unifying surrender in which the human and the divine are inextricably intertwined. In the simultaneous activation of the three virtues, God's self-giving and human participation become a living reality. Consequently, the three virtues are really one. Each individual virtue without the others cannot exist as human participation in the life of God.

Virtues express themselves in actions but they may not be considered as identical with individual actions. Virtues are personality traits which grow and develop through personal dedication. They diminish through personal negligence or counter-activities. This development takes place when there is a constructive personal development in an interhuman relationship of constructive giving and receiving. The decrease takes place when the individual tries to become his/her own source and good and makes other persons mere objects for personal satisfaction.

The whole approach to Christian life (i.e., human life in the perspective of Christ's calling) must be based upon the presence of faith, hope and love, as the participation in Christ's life. Through daily living this Christ-life develops and deepens.

HONESTY AND JUSTICE: TRUTH IN INTERHUMAN RELATIONSHIPS

I mentioned earlier that the human being, created in the image of God, is by essence a relational being. Creation itself is a relationship because it is a reaching out to another. Creation is a constructive self-communication on the part of God and therefore it asks for a constructive response on the part of the human. This constructive human response must take place in the human reality of every day. A relationship with the invisible God remains imaginary unless it translates itself in one way or another into concrete and perceptible human expressions.

The constructive human response to God is in its deepest essence an activation of the human potential to reach out constructively to others. A constructive reaching out means that the other person becomes more deeply him/herself because of this individual's action. Perhaps the clearest example of this may be seen in a couple's relationship in marriage. Both man and woman develop a deeper respect for their own personal identity and dignity because of the love they experience from each other. Their love is a constructive reaching out to each other. It is an activation in human form of the creative reaching out of God to humanity. Even if the couple does not think of this explicitly, their relationship is nonetheless a sharing in the life of God which is communicated to them in the continuous act of creation.

One of the most fundamental requirements for a constructive relationship is the presence of truth in every aspect of the human activity. Human interchange is always a two-way street. Both persons give and both receive. The giving is a presentation of oneself to the other, and at the same time it is a response to the self-revelation of the other. Man and woman in marriage present themselves to each other in the innumerable ways which manifest respect and love. In the same actions they respond to each other. This exchange can only be truly constructive when the self-presentation reflects the true self. It is honesty which demands that each individual present the truth and recognize the truth.

The recognition of truth demands a response to truth which is equally honest and which gives to the other person a constructive response. This is a matter of justice. In justice an individual recognizes the good and the needs in others and responds accordingly.

From a certain point of view, one might say that this exchange in honesty and justice is basically a mere human interaction and is a "natural" virtue, i.e., a good quality which belongs to the human condition. If we accept that the human being is created in the image of God then we may say that the participation in the life of God also belongs to the human condition. The fact that certain qualities are a gratuitous gift of God does not make them less human. Thus honesty and justice are basic requirements for human interaction and they are simultaneously expressive of the divine reality of the relationship of God to mankind.

Honesty and justice, as other aspects of human wholeness, express themselves according to the structure of the personality. Undoubtedly, the degree of self-acceptance and the experience of personal acceptability plays an important role in the expression of honesty and justice. It will be very difficult for an individual to reflect honestly and openly a poor self-image. A person will be understandably afraid to reveal oneself if earlier experiences have conveyed the message that one's personality is not acceptable to others. Because of fear a person may hide his/her identity and eventually even be confused about it.

Without a deep sense of truth, a person will be afraid of self revelation. Intimate relationships become impossible when one does not dare to reveal one's proper self to others. Thus relationships remain external. No open sharing can be expected, nor will it be possible to come to an integrated personality. Every aspect and every stage of human development is related to the sense and to the degree of honesty and justice; yet, it would seem that the deepest form in which honesty and justice is experienced is directly related to the developmental stage of industry vs. inferiority.

In this fourth stage of the psycho-socio development, the individual needs to experience his/her personal value through the production of external activity. The activity is the honest expression of his/her inner self. If this is accepted, there will be a pride in honest self-expression. If this is not accepted, there will be a fear of self-expression and a need to search for forms which are acceptable, even if these are not accurate expressions of the self. Thus, both in the manifestation of self and in the response to this manifestation the individual learns to slant the truth. Obviously, this happens in degrees and it does not happen necessarily, but the innate urge for self-preservation may not be underestimated. This urge will place its mark on every aspect of life.

If during this stage of integrating activity and personal value the individual experiences acceptance and respect, honesty and justice will increase considerably. On the other hand, if an individual learns to trust God and to accept him/herself honestly in the perspective of the call from God, honesty and justice in interhuman relationships will increase and develop. It will be the experience that true human development brings greater closeness to God while deeper respect for God creates a healthier human being.

TEMPERANCE, BALANCED RESPONSE TO LIFE

To be limited does not only mean that qualities and capacities cover certain restricted areas or that abilities are easily exhausted in their performance. To be limited also means that it is very difficult if not impossible to oversee and to evaluate adequately all the dimensions of the human personality at the same time. Consequently, there is often an inclination to overstress one particular quality or to center on one specific kind of satisfaction at the cost of other qualities or forms of satisfaction. Such a one-sided emphasis is an understandable means to counteract a deeper sense of personal insecurity. In the final analysis, however, this may lead to a distortion of the personality.

To counterbalance a one-sided inclination demands a certain restriction of this inclination. The effort to keep oneself in a balanced approach to life and self-realization often demands not doing certain things one would like to do. One has to temper oneself on that point. Hence, the temperance which is practiced is easily seen as a renouncing of what is pleasant rather than as a positive contribution to the development of other qualities. Yet, temperance is precisely that. It is the effort to balance the fulfillment of inclinations and the development of qualities which seem less attractive at this moment.

This is the point where virtue enters. Every human being is called to develop his/her human potential as fully as possible. A one-sided development could be a distorted development and could place the value of life on secondary aspects of human existence. An example of this could be an overemphasis on food. To eat is a great value and is indispensable for human existence, but to eat at the detriment of one's health would be harmful. Similarly, intellectual development is very important, but to study at the cost of kindness and understanding for others would distort the human wholeness. In both instances a certain degree of restraint is needed, not as a negative value but as a positive restoration of balance.

Temperance is an important dimension of truth. It prevents overemphasis and misrepresentation of specific qualities and of human wholeness. It contributes to an accurate expression of human relationships with God, not because of renouncing certain pleasures, but because of contributing to the development of the fulfillment of all personal qualities.

The need for balance extends itself over the full realm of human existence. From the earliest age each individual needs the development of self-acceptance which realistically combines personal values with personal limitations. The same need for balance is felt in adult life where personal sharing must remain within the limits of constructive self-communication. An unwarranted pouring out of one's personal problems is no real sharing of oneself and it can often be harmful to the listener. Balance in self-expression is not a limitation in sharing but rather a manifestation of respect for oneself and for others.

A perfect balance is never a static reality. It is rather a dynamic dimension of human life. It is a human dynamic which demands simultaneously a confidence in personal identity and a sensitivity for the values and the needs of others. This balance is in a constant process of growth. However, its basic direction and form seems to be closely related to the form of the personal identity of the individual. The person who is convinced of a personal value for society at large will make a serious effort to act accordingly. The person who conceives him/herself as a rebel or as a criminal will also act accordingly. The balance in one's self-expression will be in accord with one's self-concept.

If the form of temperance and one's personal identity are so closely related we may assume that the shape and the form in which temperance expresses itself will be greatly influenced by the individual's search for identity. This means a close relationship with the fifth stage of psycho-socio development which centers around the search for identity and identity diffusion. In this stage, the individual develops a perception of reality in which personal life is a value. According to this value, the individual develops a sense of personal acceptability, or perhaps a need to continuously prove him/herself. The need to prove oneself creates the tendency to overdo specific things.

Obviously, the search for identity is not an isolated aspect in the human being. It is a search which is always present but which is more pronounced in adolescence. Consequently, the virtue of temperance belongs to every stage of human development and is itself continuously formed. Its most pronounced form and direction, however, will be derived from the time of this most intensified search for identity.

If temperance is understood as a search for balance in full human development and if it is accepted as a necessary element for God's self-expression in the human reality, then the virtue of temperance becomes a major factor in the human search for identity. Simultaneously, the discovery of one's personal identity will be an indispensable factor in the development of a balanced self-expression. Thus, the religious perspective of the human vocation is not simply a grace which is added at a specific time. This religious perspective is as much the activation of the deepest layers in the personality.

GENEROSITY, CONSTRUCTIVE SELFGIVING

Human life is dynamic. This means it is in a constant process of self-preservation, development, and self-extension. Human life is also relational. This means that it finds its origin, its development and its fulfillment in reaching out to others and receiving from them. Combining these two essential qualities we may say that "relational dynamics" is one of the most important aspects of human life and development. As an inter-human perspective, relational dynamics begin at the earliest stages of human life and continue their activity until life is completed in the action of dying.

As a perspective of being created in the image of God the relational dynamics are present and active at every moment of human existence. At every moment the human being is in the process of self-realization and thus gives a concrete expression to the presence (or the absence) of God's creative love. It is, however, largely the human choice as to what extent this relational dynamics reaches out to others or is self-directed.

Some persons feel at ease, find happiness and fulfillment when they can contribute to the happiness of others, particularly when this contribution means a personal involvement. For these persons, such forms of personal involvement are expressions of respect for others and of personal enrichment. Other persons seem to be exactly the opposite. Involvement with others seems to be experienced as threatening. They feel safe behind the walls they build around themselves, or when they can dominate others and utilize them to enhance their personal importance. It is not uncommon that these persons give much of what they have to assist other people, but their giving is material and external rather than an expression of personal concern for others.

There are great differences in the way people give and can give. Sometimes, giving creates new depths in the receiver; in other instances, giving has a restrictive and suffocating effect. This is not simply a matter of dealing with good or bad personalities. It is rather a dealing with different personalities who express themselves in their own way. They all can be generous in their own way and they can be quite honest in their generosity. Yet while the generosity of some is liberating, the generosity of others is confining. At the root of this difference lies the individual's self-image and the perception of self-worth.

Genuine self-giving demands a self-acceptance which not only perceives the personality as valuable, but which also feels at ease in reaching out to others. A fearful person is not only afraid to be rejected if his/her personality were known to others but this person is also unable to allow others to contribute to his/her development. The influence of others is experienced as a threat to one's personality. A self-accepting person experiences his/her own existence as a value and wants to offer this value to others. Therefore, a self-accepting person can be intimate with others. Intimacy means allowing oneself to be known by others and, at the same time, allowing others to contribute to the deepening of one's own personality.

A self-accepting person is able and willing to share with others in a loving exchange which deepens relationships. It is a sharing and giving which does not bind into submission, but which liberates for personal growth. Yet, in this increased freedom a stronger bond of unity is established.

The relational dynamics of the individual with God are not different. It remains the personality structure which activates and expresses itself. The personality structure is the form in which the generosity of the creator is translated into the human dimensions of this person. Sometimes it is more complete than other times even if the individual is always as generous as he/she can be. Greater human happiness and freedom, however, is found where deeper self-giving is possible. So also, a deeper relationship with God is possible when the individual is capable of listening more generously to God's call and responding to it more freely.

The virtue of generosity, therefore, seems to express itself in the form and balance of the individual's tension between the search for intimacy and isolation. This does not mean that the virtue of generosity originates at this point. A degree of listening to God and responding to his call is present at any stage of human development, but the form in which it is expressed is more clearly manifested in the developmental tension of intimacy vs. isolation.

The more generous a person can be with his/her fellow human beings, the deeper one's response to God can be.

Reversely, the experience and understanding of God's generosity for humanity inspires greater generosity toward one's fellowmen. The experience of God's generosity is a deepening of the awareness of personal value. The sense of personal value has a liberating influence upon human self-expression with one's fellow human beings as well as with God.

FORTITUDE, LOVE DESPITE HARDSHIP

Earlier I described creation as a continuous self-communication of God and as God's self-expression in a new, original form. This self-expression in created perceptible form we have called "human." God's actions, as far as we can understand them, are instantaneous. Their completion does not demand a lapse of time. In human self-realization this is different. Human activity is always time-measured. Yet, human self-realization is a participation in the life of the creator. It is a participation in God's self-expression, and therefore, it is a participation in creation. It is, however, creation in slow-motion.

This time-measured aspect of human activity has many consequences. It means that human wholeness is not contained in one individual action. Nor is the human attitude and direction of the personality expressed in one single moment. The acceptance of oneself is a life-process and constructive interhuman relationship demands a certain amount of time to deepen and ripen. Love is not a once in a life-time self-giving nor can one act of love express the fullness of personal dedication. Intimacy is not achieved in one act of pouring out one's deeper feelings. Intimacy demands a careful, trusting but cautious feeling one's way into the life of another person.

Human growth and development demands perseverance. In human activity one encounters monotony and fatigue. One must be ready to repeat the same action over and over again in seemingly the same circumstances, or to express oneself in new ways. People change and one needs to adapt even when fatigue has drained one's energy. Full human development is impossible without strength and courage; it demands self-respect and unselfishness.

These qualities are required at every period of time between birth and old age. However, they seem to be more explicitly needed when the period of external growth and change has passed and when one extends oneself in the slow process of self-communication while waiting for the growth of those to whom one has given oneself. Continuous courage and strength are the mark of the adult who understands the purpose of life and has experienced its difficulties, yet is determined to live its value.

This form of conscious and personal application to the goal and purpose of life despite difficulties is the specific meaning and form of the virtue of fortitude. Fortitude is a human virtue because it enables the individual to continue his/her response to the constant demands of growth and development. Fortitude overcomes monotony and farigue without losing sight of sensitivity and concern.

For the same reasons, fortitude is also a Christian virtue. The expression of God's creative presence and goodness goes through the same slow processes as human growth and development. It suffers the same hardships in the continuous task of personal dedication. As a Christian virtue, however, fortitude has the advantage of joining the strength of the divine presence to the limited human endurance. Fortitude gathers the earlier experience of personal acceptability, of personal confidence and of value for others into one vision of personal wholeness. In this vision the individual can see oneself as a source of value for self-expression. This personal vision is not only a vision on the interhuman relationships and development, but also on the human reality which expresses the presence of God.

Fortitude not only touches all of human life, it also touches every virtue in human and Christian existence. Wherever development and growth are part of human existence there the virtue of fortitude plays an indispensable role. As a Christian virtue it is not an addition to human strength. It is rather a depth-dimension and form which makes human perseverance fully human. Fortitude is the continuous and undiminished creative power of God translated into the process of human development.

PRUDENCE, INTELLIGENT RISK-TAKING

Human life is filled with surprises. Some are pleasant, some are painful; some are edifying, others are emotionally upsetting. It is one of the characteristics of surprises that they cannot be predicted. Another of their characteristics is that they frequently are the source of vibrancy, of growth and of depth.

Life as a relational reality is always more or less unpredictable. Many aspects of our own life are beyond our control. Unintended things happen to us, some pleasant, some unpleasant, but whatever their value these new circumstances demand a readjustment in our life. If we cannot predict what will happen to our own person, still less can we predict the circumstances in the lives of others. Yet, our relational existence is inextricably interwoven with the lives of many people. Here too we continuously need to readjust.

In interhuman relationships one can try to follow familiar and tested procedures in order to avoid surprises. One may succeed to a certain extent to predict the outcome of such an approach, but one also confines oneself to a static form of self-expression which has little growth or development. Life becomes then the opposite of a dynamic relationship. It is also possible to go to the other extreme and act upon every impulse without taking into account past experiences. In this approach, every thing is a surprise. One may wonder, however, how constructive this is since it seems to disregard much of the abilities acquired through earlier experiences.

Between the attitudes of extreme fearfulness and uncritical impulsivity lies a balance which evaluates both the past and the future. This balance evaluates the past by knowing and accepting the abilities which one has developed. The individual knows in which circumstances he/she is more likely to succeed or to fail. The past has shown his/her personal strength and weaknesses, and above all, the individual has learned to accept him/herself as a valuable person who is capable within certain limits. To know one's limits is not experienced as a depreciation of one's value but as a description of the terrain within which the personality is good and acceptable.

By looking from the past to the present, this individual can project the future. This projection is not a certitude of what is going to be or of what can be done. It is a projection of what his/her personal abilities can accomplish under favorable circumstances. Past experiences have conveyed a sense of personal value and dignity which is not dependent on success. Though failure may be painful, it is usually not experienced as destructive. The experience of the past have also taught one that the most satisfactory growth takes place within the full activation of one's potential, even when such action involves an element of risk.

In continuous self-activation the individual learns his/her own efficiency in all sorts of situations. One also develops a clear vision of one's goal and destiny. There seems to be an attitude in which the information and experiences of the past jell together into one integrated expression of human wholeness. In plain human terminology we usually call the approach to life of such a person a prudent approach to life. There is caution without fear, courage without audacity and strength without disdain.

These qualities belong to human self-expression in relation to God's self-manifestation in the human reality. All the human qualities in the form and in the degree of their development are involved when individual persons want their human life to be an expression of God's goodness and creative presence. The human being who is fully alive knows that God's presence is not primarily manifested by the static observance of external commandments. God's presence is manifested in the spontaneous activation of human goodness and creative self-giving.

On the basis of the active presence of faith, hope and love, shaped in truth, balance and personal generosity, the individual can take the risk of growing. The virtue of prudence has all the characteristics of human prudence, but in addition to this, it has also the perspective of the divine vocation in human life. This dimension of human wholeness makes the perspective of life more complete. Without changing human prudence, the virtue of prudence deepens all its human dimensions. Human prudence grows through the touch of divine wisdom (through the vision in the perspective of God's presence). Simultaneously, divine wisdom is more fully grasped because of a deeper development of human qualities.

Vatican Council II states that "only in the mystery of the Incarnate Word can the mystery of man take on light." Similarly, only through a deeper grasp of the wonder of human existence can we develop a greater appreciation of the mystery of the Incarnation. If Incarnation means that in Jesus, God participated in the human reality in order to bring to the human reality participation in the life of God, then we must be able to find God when we study the human, and discover the human when we study God.

If this is true, then there can be no dichotomy between honest human self-activation and God's self-manifestation. The fullness of the presence of God must then be recognized in the fullness of human self-expression according to the individual's present ability. Perfection does not exist in flawlessness according to human measurements, but in the totality of personal application at any given moment of one's existence. Holiness or wholeness is not achieved through faithful observance of laws, but Human and Christian wholeness is established in the creative tension between the developmental processes of personality structures and Christian virtues. In this tension we find the degree in which God is allowed to manifest himself in human life, and the degree in which the human allows himself to be united with God.

Diagram 4 is the last progressive step after diagrams 1, 2 and 3. The circular presentation intends to show the interconnection of the virtues among themselves. Their location in relation to the stages of psycho-socio crises, criteria for mental health and ethical modalities indicates the structure, tension and balance of the personality from which the individual virtues seem to derive their form. This relationship does not indicate their origin or their primary field of concern and operation. All the virtues operate at any period of life or stage of development where a person can take individual responsibility. However, the external shape of the virtues is influenced by a specific stage of personality structure. In turn, this specific personality structure is more likely to benefit by the development and

growth of specific virtues. For instance, faith will largely be
shaped by the degree of basic trust, while basic trust will be
the first personality structure to benefit by the development
of faith.

Diagram 5a & 5b present a different view on the interaction of the stages of personality development and
Christian virtues. It is a linear presentation in which the
diagonal arrangement of the successive stages of
development indicates their epigenetic nature. Each stage
is, in a certain form and degree, present in all earlier and
subsequent stages. The location in one square of the four
different aspects of the personality, psycho-socio crisis,
criterion for mental health, ethical modality and Christian
virtue is meant to show the form or shape of each aspect but
not its limited or primary field of operation.

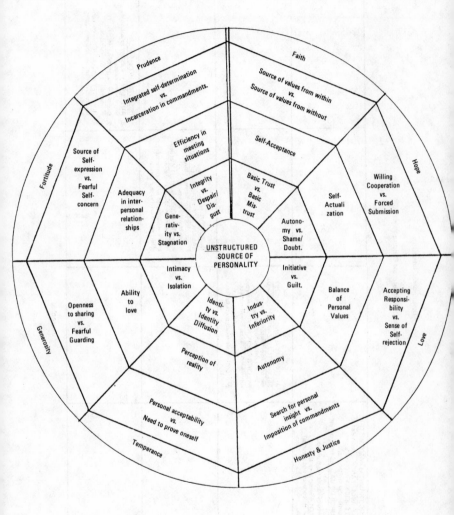

Diagram 4

Developmental Interaction

Personality Structures and Christian Virtues

I.
<u>Infancy</u>
(0-1 yr.)
	1. BASIC THRUST vs BASIC MISTRUST
	2. SELF-ACCEPTANCE — ability to accept and to live with one's own potential and limitations.
	3. SOURCE OF VALUES from within
	      vs
	   Source of values from without
	4. FAITH — integrative acceptance of total dependence and personal value.		

II. <u>Childhood</u> (1-3 yrs.)		1. AUTONOMY vs SHAME or DOUBT 2. SELF-ACTUALIZATION — potential and urge to activate one's capacities in relation to others. 3. WILLING COOPERATION vs forced submission with loss of self-respect. 4. HOPE — acceptance of limitations with confidence of ultimate fulfillment.	
III. <u>Play Age</u> (3-6 yrs.)			1. INITIATIVE vs GUILT 2. BALANCE OF PERSONAL VALUES — integrating factor between inner values and external expression. 3. Accepting RESPONSIBILITY vs Self-rejection when taking initiative. 4. LOVE — ability of self-commitment; giving and receiving as a person.
IV. <u>School Age</u> (6-12 yrs.)			1. INDUSTRY vs INFERIORITY 2. AUTONOMY — ability to act on a set of inner values. 3. Search for PERSONAL INSIGHTS vs imposition of commandments. 4. HONESTY and JUSTICE — concern for truth in doctrine and self-expression.

Diagram 5a

Developmental Interaction
Personality Structures and Christian Virtues

V. Adolescence (12-18 yrs.)	1. IDENTITY vs IDENTITY DIFFUSION 2. PERCEPTION OF REALITY – freedom from emotional distortion; respect for others. 3. Sense of PERSONAL ACCEPTABIL-ITY vs Need to prove oneself. 4. TEMPERANCE – search for balance in the activation of personal qualities for the good of self and others.		
VI. Young Adult (19-25 yrs.)	1. INTIMACY vs ISOLATION 2. ABILITY TO LOVE – constructive self-giving to others; response to others without exploitation. 3. OPENNESS TO SHARING vs Fearful guarding. 4. GENEROSITY – availability of one's total self for the good of others without fear of loss of self.		
VII. Adulthood (25-40 yrs.)		1. GENERATIVITY vs STAGNATION/ SELF-ABSORPTION 2. ADEQUACY IN INTERPERSONAL RELATIONSHIPS – aggressiveness without dominance. 3. Source of SELF-EXPRESSION vs fearful self-concern 4. FORTITUDE – creative perseverance in building self and mankind.	
VIII. Mature Age (40 · · · · up)			1. INTEGRITY vs DESPAIR, DISGUST 2. EFFICIENCY IN MEETING SITUA-TIONS and capacity for adaptation 3. INTEGRATED SELF-DETERMINA-TION vs Incarceration in commandments. 4. PRUDENCE – ability to grasp wholeness and to act constructively.

Diagram 5b:

FOOTNOTES

CHAPTER ONE

1. van der Poel, Rev. Cornelius J., Religious Life: A Risk of Love. Dimension Books, Denville, N.Y. 1972, Pp. 13-19.
2. Godin, Rev. Andre., The Pastor as Counselor, Holt, Rinehart, Winston. New York, N.Y. 1965. Pp. 17-20.

CHAPTER TWO

1. Erikson, Erik H., Identity and the Life Cycle. Psychological Issues Vol. I, n. 1. International University Press, Inc. New York, N.Y. 1959, Pp. 50-100.
2. Erikson, Erik H., Reflections on Dr. Borg's Life Cycle. *Daedalus* Spring 1976, p. 23.
3. Erikson, Erik H., Identity and the Life Cycle. p. 68.
4. Op. Cit. p. 82.
5. Op. Cit. p. 89.

CHAPTER THREE

1. Davis, Charles, Body as Spirit. Seabury Press, New York, N.Y. 1976, p. 13.
2. Fromm Erich, The Art of Loving. Bantam Books (pb.) 1963, Pp. 22ff.

CHAPTER FOUR

1. Kohlberg, Lawrence, Stages of Moral Development as a Basis for Moral Education. In "Moral Education.

Interdisciplinary   Approaches.''   Beck/
Crittenden/Sullivan, ed. Newman Press, New York,
N.Y. 1971, Pp. 23-92.
2. Piaget, Jean, The Moral Judgment of the Child. The
   Free Press, New York, N.Y. 1969.

CHAPTER FIVE

1. Pastoral Constitution on the Church in the Modern
   World. n. 22.
2. fan der Poel, Cornelius J., The Search for Human
   Values. Paulist/Newman Press, 1971, Pp. 146ff.
3. Rahner, Karl, in Sacramentum Mundi, Vol. 2, p. 311.
4. Ibid.
5. New (Dutch) Catechism. Herder & Herder, New York,
   N.Y. 1967, p. 197.
6. Kerstiens, Ferdinand, in Sacramentum Mundi, Vol. 3
   p. 64.
7. Op. Cit. p. 62.

CHAPTER SIX

1. Rahner, Karl, Christian at the Crossroads. Seabury
   Press, New York, N.Y. 1975. p. 51.
2. Ibid.